SEVEN YEAR INTERLUDE

Eric J Blakemore

MINERVA PRESS
MONTREUX LONDON WASHINGTON

SEVEN YEAR INTERLUDE
Copyright © Eric J Blakemore 1995

All Rights Reserved

No part of this book may be reproduced in any form,
by photocopying or by any electronic or mechanical means,
including information storage or retrieval systems,
without permission in writing from both the copyright owner
and the publisher of this book.

ISBN 1 85863 446 6

First Published 1995 by
MINERVA PRESS
1 Cromwell Place
London SW7 2JE

Printed in Great Britain by
B.W.D. Ltd., Northolt, Middlesex

SEVEN YEAR INTERLUDE

ABOUT THE AUTHOR

Eric Blakemore was born in June 1919 in Timperley, a small village in Cheshire. His parents moved to London in 1921, where he spent his maturing years in North London. He was educated at private schools until 11 years, then Minchenden Secondary School and University Tutorial College. On leaving college, he studied Accountancy until joining the Royal Air Force.

Leaving the R.A.F. in June 1946, he entered the Accounting profession on the commercial side. He married his wife Lily in 1948. They have two sons, Philip a Banking official and David a Chartered Surveyor.

In 1984, he retired from his position as Financial Controller with an American subsidiary. He now spends his leisure hours playing golf, gardening and engaging in other hobbies.

CONTENTS

		Page
Foreword and Dedication		ix
Chapter 1	Introduction	11
Chapter 2	1939	12
Chapter 3	1940	15
Chapter 4	1941	22
Chapter 5	1942-43	34
Chapter 6	1944	44
Chapter 7	1945	68
Chapter 8	1946	79
Chapter 9	Conclusion	81
Footnote		86
Appendices		87

Foreword and Dedication

In writing this book, I am carrying out a promise that I made to myself many years ago and giving my thoughts an airing. If I sound sometimes too critical it is only because I feel that many Bomber crews were sent on missions with the odds stacked against them, and even though Guy Gibson in his book "Enemy Coast Ahead" says that losses on any one air raid are not unduly high (rarely above ten per cent), I wonder how long the Navy or Army would have lasted with average losses like that. I therefore dedicate this book to the Air and Ground crews of Bomber Command for their bravery/courage and dedication; also, on a personal note, to two girls, Betty Pontin and Jean Nicoll, who, unknown to them, helped to keep my spirits high when things looked black, with the belief that I was doing my little bit to protect them (and of course my family), from the horror of defeat and Occupation. And last, but not least, to the Dutch Resistance and others, without whose brave help, I would probably not be writing these memoirs.

I should also like to thank Nancy de Vries, one of my Dutch helpers, for typing the original script and helping with the recollection of some of my experiences when in Holland. Also, I thank Max Hastings for allowing me to quote from his excellent book "Bomber Command".

CHAPTER 1

Introduction

What is an interlude? According to the Oxford Dictionary, it is a break in a play, orchestral concert or an interval in an activity. The activity I am concerned with is life as a civilian and, therefore to me, the period in uniform during the Second World War, which was an interlude that for millions changed their whole way of life, or in many regrettable cases meant the end of life as we know it. I am Eric J. Blakemore. "Who is he?" most people would say. Actually, no one of any significance, just one of the many young people who were around in 1939, with a background in my case of a fairly comfortable family upbringing in North London, with my three sisters, two elder, one younger; so maybe a little spoilt. My early education was at small private schools up to the 11 plus examination (due to having contracted Rheumatic Fever when six years old, leaving me a little delicate). I then attended Senior School at Minchenden Secondary School, Southgate followed by a period at University Tutorial College, and then on to two years' training to be an Accountant, until the Call Up.

I have recounted my experience in uniform under the separate years 1940-1946, trying to show the serious and sad side of service life, along with the amusing and sometimes inspiring episodes which brought friendship and understanding, impossible to find in any other walk of life.

The final chapter is a long hard look at what effect the seven years have had on my life with the resulting gains and losses; plus my comments and thoughts on various publications and statements regarding the roll of Bomber Command in the War.

CHAPTER 2

1939

The year started as perhaps it was meant to with the wintry weather bringing a cold shiver to most of the population. Uppermost in everyone's thoughts when the new year was ushered in was "Peace in our Time". At least we hoped so, though the general feeling was that the piece of paper held up by Neville Chamberlain the previous year on returning from Germany after meeting Hitler, would only enable us to mark time while we prepared.

Life continued in very much the same way for the early part of the year, apart from the announcement of National Service for certain age groups. It was in March after Germany's entry into Czechoslovakia, that the feeling was they would not stop there, and something would happen during the coming months. Service displays were now taking place in the City, encouraging recruitment for regular or voluntary service.

The most serious pointer to some of us was the digging of trenches across the putting greens at Lincoln Inn Fields, so stopping our lunch time activity. I had in the meantime completed the forms to join the Royal Air Force Volunteer Reserve as aircrew and awaited acceptance hopefully.

Despite the preparations in case of war, I would not say there was an air of gloom about. On the contrary, apart from the apprehension, we all continued whatever activities interested us. There were visits to the Cup Final to see Pompey beat the Wolves, and another to Lords on Whit Monday for the Middlesex v. Sussex Cricket to see how many runs Denis Compton would make, or how many wickets Jack Nye would take for Sussex (Jack had been one of my coaches at Alan Fairfax's Indoor Cricket School). Actually Denis made 81 and Jack took 3 wickets. There was a visit to Wimbledon for the first Saturday's tennis, in my case to see Jean Nicoll, one of Britain's up and coming stars. I was one of her many fans, and in fact she wore some white heather I sent her (which unfortunately brought Jean little luck). There were, finally, visits to the Speedway, both cycle and roller, at Harringay, not to mention the cinema, and theatre, which continued in a summer which weather wise was, if my memory serves me right, above average.

The only storm clouds I remember were those gathering over Eastern Europe as August came to its close. It was with no great surprise, only regret, that we heard the Prime Minister on Sunday 3rd September declare that we were at war.

Within half an hour the sirens were sounding and we wondered what we were in for. It was a false alarm and the same happened that night. As my Father was a schoolmaster, he was evacuated with his school to Essex; my Mother and young sister Joan followed, so the family was broken up, and that would be the last time the six of us were together. Thus the war was already affecting family life for us and for many millions more.

I remember a few days later when early one sunny morning, the sirens sounded. At that time the streets had to be kept clear, so no one left their homes. It only lasted an hour and it was an amazing sight to see on the sounding of the "all clear", nearly everyone setting off for work at the same time. From every gate a resident was emerging, making his or her way to the station. It was like one of today's television adverts. To make the situation more chaotic, on arrival at Southgate Underground Station, it was announced that no trains were running, and no explanation was given. This gave rise to all sorts of rumours about bombs being dropped and places being destroyed. Actually the hold up was due to a train's shoe overheating and welding itself to the live rail; it was a good example as to how rumours start and become exaggerated and distorted. The alert had been a false alarm anyway.

The weeks that followed were a period of apprehension. Along with the black out, all places of entertainment were closed, the radio was mostly organ music and news, so the only activity was going to work and getting home.

The restrictions were soon lifted and the phoney war was over in that sport was resumed on a restricted basis, and the cinemas and theatres reopened, strangely enough not to very full houses.

It was rather amazing how everyone seemed to quickly fall into the new routine, with the black out, the carrying of gas masks, the evacuation of children, not to mention the reporting for full time duty of Service, Police, Air Raid Wardens and many other categories. I was called for my medical in the month of November, which was an experience in itself. I had volunteered for flying duties with the Royal

Air Force, and, when mentioning that I had had rheumatic fever when young, I was surrounded by a team of doctors to see if it was possible that I could be A1. It was, and they could only state what a dedicated doctor I must have had during my illness. (Right up to the introduction of the National Health scheme, doctors attended their patients in hospital).

I was very pleased at the result of the medical and was now looking forward to my call-up papers. Studying and training had become a little difficult and it was hard to give the time and concentration needed.

I went home to my parents (who, with my younger sister, were now living in Bournemouth) for Christmas and New Year, wondering like everyone else what 1940 would bring forth, and how different our future would be.

CHAPTER 3

1940

The year opened quietly with the continuation of the so called phoney war, yet 1940 was to be one of the most important years in the history of the British Isles, even of the rest of the world, the year when Germany, alongside Japan and Italy, could have been on the road to ruling the world.

I received my call up papers in January for flying duties as Radio Operator/Air Gunner with the Royal Air Force, to report in three weeks' time. I thought that a week at home before reporting would be a nice relaxation, but on requesting this from my employers, I was quickly informed that I could not expect favours and should carry on training until the last moment. (I must point out that I left a week early anyway and took a week's holiday!)

So the day arrived for me to report for duty and start my new life. How I felt as I travelled up from Bournemouth is hard to describe: apprehension maybe, but more relief that at last the waiting was over, and I could now settle down to make my contribution towards the war effort.

No. 1 R.A.F. Receiving Centre Uxbridge was my reporting base and as I walked along Uxbridge High Street my thoughts were full of questions which would soon be answered in the following years. Standing at the entrance were the R.A.F. Police who, on approaching, said just one word: "Recruit?" I nodded, to which after inspecting my reporting papers, they said, "Come on in." So began the seven year interlude.

There were over one hundred other recruits that day and we were all collected in a hall and given instructions as to what would take place in the next few days.

We were shown our barrack room where we were allocated a bed and locker, and after a clean up were taken for the main meal, which I actually thought was very reasonable. In the afternoon the oath was taken en masse and then down to the kitting out store, where we were supplied with uniform, clothes and enough equipment to fill a kitbag.

On returning to the sleeping quarters we were instructed to change into our uniforms and pack our civilian clothes ready to be sent home.

The next two days were spent with lectures about the R.A.F. and a series of inoculations and vaccinations, and perhaps more importantly, a pay parade where everyone received ten shillings.

These few days were a whole new experience for me, the first taste of communal life, having never been to boarding school, camps etc., plus always having had my own room at home.

Surprisingly this had little effect, due mainly to being ready for sleep each night after the day's activities, as well as being in the company of the same age group, all starting a new life.

On the third day we were informed that we would be carrying out our initial four weeks' training at Morecambe and would travel by special train from Uxbridge that evening.

We were all lined up with our kit bags to march to the station and, as an extra, each was issued with a rifle; they were needed up at Morecambe for the training. So we had a rifle for the left arm and a kit bag for the right; the only trouble was that the jabs we had received were now taking effect and our left arms were useless, so you can imagine the chaos that ensued. All along the route rifles and kit bags were being dropped as arms gave out, which resulted in the N.C.O.s in charge having to carry the rifles. The only amusing part of the march was the helpful advice from passing motorists, cyclists and, not least, from bus conductors with their cockney humour. I remember one N.C.O. stating that he would have us carrying two kit bags by the time he was finished. Little did we know how true that would be in later months!

Our journey up to Morecambe was uneventful. We were too tired to do anything other than sleep and eventually arrived around eleven o'clock the next morning. We were assembled in front of the station and marched through the streets to be detailed off to different prearranged billets, mostly guest houses. The proprietors found this very acceptable, as they were in business again, although it was winter. They made us very welcome; whether they would do the same for others when the summer season arrived, I never found out. Perhaps they thought the war would be over by then.

The four weeks were spent in marching with rifle drill and physical training. The weather was very cold with the north west winds blowing along the promenades. All this exercise and fresh air, after being a city boy, resulted in always having an enormous appetite (which I retained for the larger part of my service), development of muscles and putting on at least one stone in weight; strangely this was to be the only organised physical exercise I had in my service life. The drill and exercise were certainly good for the physical side. Mentally, I am not too sure what the object of the instructor seemed to be, as to shout, swear and generally to belittle and humiliate any individual who was not up to their standard was, to my mind, a strange way to get the best out of anyone or encourage them in a different way of life. I also noticed that it was the higher educated, or upper class (what a horrible description), who seemed to bear the brunt of this sadistic verbal assault.

Apart from further jabs, the only painful memories are of doing arm presses in the Winter Gardens car park which was covered in loose cinders. The town itself was a fairly quiet place, except for Saturdays, when there was a large influx of girls from outer areas. I think a good time was had by all, though on two shillings a day, it was not easy! The only town that was not out of bounds was Lancaster. We made a visit one Sunday morning and the place was deserted, not a person to be seen; everyone obviously had a long lie in on Sundays.

The four weeks quickly passed and we were ready to move on to our next posting. Due to the courses for training radio operators being full at the time, the half dozen of us waiting for the course were posted to No. 1 Apprentice School at Halton, Bucks, to carry out general duties.

For the next few weeks we were to have the experience of an R.A.F. station where strict discipline was of the highest order; a good grounding for a five week recruit, it kept you on your toes. The war was still in its phoney stage and life at Halton was very much as in peace time. How quickly this was to change in the next few months. This extreme discipline, plus lack of flexibility, showed itself when, after being granted my first leave, I decided to catch the first train from Wendover to town. I reported at 6 a.m. to collect my leave pass from the guard room, but was quickly told I would have to wait until Reveille, which was 6.30 a.m., the start of my pass; so I was made to stand around and wait, resulting in a missed connection.

The one outstanding episode while at Halton was the high standard set by a young member of the Woman's Auxiliary Air Force who gave her life in saving a child being run down by a motor vehicle. She threw herself in front and pushed the child to safety. This tragedy took place in Aylesbury, a few miles from Halton. The funeral befitting for the occasion was military and held at Halton, the burial taking place in the local cemetery. This was the first experience that would make the wearing of a uniform a matter of pride.

Our duties were varied and to say the least mundane and uninteresting, being only lightened by the chance to walk and see the lovely countryside around the camp. The weather was already showing itself to be the start of a long hot summer.

A few weeks later the Germans started their Blitz Krieg offence and advanced rapidly across the low countries. The phoney war was ended and the real action was to start and last for the next five years.

Towards the end of May our posting came through and we were on our way to No. 2 E & W School Yatesbury, Wilts. The retreat from the beaches of France was on and it was while waiting for a connection, that a train full of soldiers from the beaches pulled in across the line. Being in R.A.F. uniform, we received a fair amount of abuse, very understandable in the circumstances. Due to the lack of air cover over the beaches, they felt the R.A.F. had let them down. Later the Battle of Britain would explain their absence.

Yatesbury is in the middle of the Wiltshire downs alongside the Old Bath Road, and one of our first duties was to dig trenches in the chalk around the camp and the water tower up on the hill, very hard work especially with the very hot weather, which was to last until the autumn. We at least got very tanned and retained our fitness.

The hut I was assigned to had a fantastic cross section of airmen from all walks of life. I can honestly say that we all got on like a house on fire. Amongst over 30 men we had schoolteachers, an artist, an actor, dance band musicians, a member of a well known card manufacturing firm and so on.

Work was hard, with very little time off, though eventually with the threat of invasion receding, we did get a short weekend once a month; however, most weeks the hut was half empty after classes on Saturday till Sunday night, many having gone to London.

I spent most any Sundays off visiting the towns in the vicinity: Bath, Bradford on Avon, Trowbridge, Frome, Calne, etc. This was quite an education as they all have such interesting buildings and history. It also alleviated the pressure of intensive studies during the other six days of the week.

It was hard to believe during that long hot summer that in the peace and tranquillity of the West country we were at war and fighting for our existence.

The camp at Yatesbury, as previously mentioned, was on the Old Bath Road A4 and was therefore easier for getting lifts than others.

Queen Mary was often seen passing on her way to Badminton and it was said, on good authority, that a few airmen were kindly given lifts by Her Majesty.

The only way I could get home was by hitching a lift across country via Devises, Salisbury, Ringwood and on to Bournemouth. I had some long walks across Salisbury plain, but on the whole was fairly lucky with regard to lifts; and at the same time I met some very interesting people, both civilian and service.

The instruction on Morse and practical radio maintenance took place in classrooms. One amusing incident still makes me smile. One civilian instructor, who was Dutch, always insisted after Morse tests on counting the number of mistakes made by his pupils and summarising on the blackboard. His request was not "hands up for no errors etc.", but always "fingers for no errors and so on." He could never understand why he always had more numbers on the board than in the class: obviously some of his pupils were putting fingers up twice, and who were the culprits? Why, the pupils who were teachers in civilian life!

One other amusing episode was a mass prank by the whole hut less one, that one being the victim, who had decided to go to bed early. After he had been asleep for two hours, the time was around 10 p.m., and we all put ourselves in various stages of dressing, shaving etc. We then woke the victim telling him to hurry or he would be late for breakfast. He instantly jumped out of bed and rushed out to the ablutions. When he returned, washed and shaved, we were all in bed ready for a night's sleep. I won't repeat the words he used but he soon saw the funny side and joined in the good laugh had by all.

We all looked forward to the flying instruction which for most of us would be our first flight. It would take place in Domine 1's, which had been on the Jersey Airways route, now fitted with radios for sending Morse over the air. We were all a little nervous on the first flight. Reactions differed as to the effect of flying. Apart from the first trip, very few suffered any ill effects; in fact, I can say that I never felt unwell when flying under any condition; actually the reverse was the case; it was always a cure for a slight hangover.

As the year advanced, the shock of the fall of France receded. I can vouch that I never met anyone, either civilian and service, who thought that defeat was possible. Optimism was always high, probably due to the strength of Winston Churchill's down to earth approach, plus the success of the fighter boys in what was "the Battle of Britain". Despite the start of the bombing by the Luftwaffe of British towns, where the victims were civilians, morale was of the highest order. In spite of a few hang ups, I passed the tests, which would qualify me as a Radio Operator after which I would then go on to an air gunnery course to obtain my wings and the three stripes. All aircrew were promoted to Sergeant on qualifying for their wings, much to the annoyance of ground crew regular airmen, who had to wait years before attaining the rank. This rankling went on for a long time until they realised and saw the rate of survival by the aircrew; more about this in a later chapter.

There was a slight delay in the posting to the air gunnery course, so a temporary posting for four of us to Coastal Command H.Q. at Chatham (deep underground) was made. We had a good journey to Chatham, as one of our colleagues had a car. We stopped off for lunch in London at a cinema restaurant, owned by his father. An air raid was in progress when we arrived in Chatham which was not surprising as they were very frequent over the Medway towns. As we made our way down one street, a mine landed at the far end. The blast lifted the car a foot off the ground and dropped it facing the other way: what a welcome! Fortunately the only other experience was when I went to the cinema one evening; my other colleagues were on duty so I was on my own. The siren situated on the top of the building sounded the alert. I noticed some people leaving but it was only at the interval that I realised I was the only person left watching, apart from the staff. If my memory serves me right, the film was 'Bluebird' with Shirley Temple.

We were very pleased when, after one week, just before Christmas, our posting to an air gunnery course came through and we were on our way to No. 9 Bombing & Gunnery school at Penrhos in North Wales. It was my first Christmas away from home and it seemed strange to be away from the family.

Having just arrived in North Wales we were not au fait with the licensing laws and we got a big disappointment when on Christmas Eve, visiting a pub just before 9 p.m. after a visit to the cinema, we were told "last drinks gentlemen." The two day break, which included an excellent Christmas dinner served by the Officers and N.C.O.s, was soon over and our concentration was set on the gunnery course. We were billeted out for sleeping only in Llandbedrog, three miles to the West, and our kind landlady was always worried she could not supply supper at night. No rations were allowed, even though it meant a round trip of three miles, sometimes in deep snow, if we required any further subsistence.

All the instruction before the New Year was in the classroom and we were very excited at the prospect of flying again, this time in Fairy Battles and Whitleys.

CHAPTER 4

1941

The New Year started with heavy falls of snow, not unusual in North Wales, and a lot of time and energy was spent in keeping the airfield clear for flying.

Intensive instruction proceeded despite the weather and we enjoyed flying in the heavier aircraft. It was a welcome change from bookwork. The exercises were firing at a drogue towed by another aircraft from a Lewis gun. We were each given an ammunition drum with the tips of the billets having different colours, which then showed the number of hits on the target, or at least it was supposed to. On one trip I had no time to fire my drum, yet still received a number of hits, which was very pleasing.

During the course we had several photographs taken by Cecil Beaton (later the court photographer and a Knight) of different aspects on the course. They later appeared in the ABC of the R.A.F. (1941).

January 31st was the day for the official passing out and presentation of wings, making us all qualified Radio Operators/Air Gunners; at least that is what we thought! As time would tell, much more was to be learned, but not in text books or lectures. A quick trip to Pwllheli to have our wings and stripes sewn on was made by most of the course.

The next posting would be to an operational training unit; crews would be mostly made up of six aircrew, i.e. two pilots, navigator, two radio operators (one for the front turret) and a rear gunner. They would then train as a unit on an aircraft already operating on the squadrons where they would be posted to, after completing the course.

We caught the night Irish Mail train to Euston. Our destination was 10 O.T.U. at Abingdon, Berkshire. The stay here was very brief. A new O.T.U. No. 21 was being formed at Moreton-in-Marsh and we were posted there. The only memories of Abingdon were of sleeping in an old glove factory in the town by the river and seeing one of the best camp shows, led by one of Billy Cotton's ex musicians.

Due to the short stay, the six of us, all radio operators/air gunners had not been allocated to any crew, so it was a new start at Moreton. They would be flying Wellingtons which was very pleasing for us. It was a great thrill to fly in these aircraft known affectionately as Wimpeys. To me they were the best aircraft produced in the war: many aircrew owed their lives (including myself on several occasions) to the amazing ability of the aircraft to keep going despite serious damage, loss of an engine, or being stripped of the fabric.

Our crew was made out of the following personnel:

- Pilots: Sergeants Vic Billett and B. G. Hawes
- Navigator: John Bruce
- Radio Operators/Air Gunners: Vic Clarke and myself
- Rear Gunner: Jim Bell

We instantly blended as a unit which was essential for survival. A crew of a bomber was a very small unit unlike the Army or the Navy, so it is difficult to make comparisons, though I know it was achieved by these services.

We were the first to take the course at Moreton, which meant a routine had not yet been formed, resulting in an enjoyable and flexible seven week course. The instructor-pupil relationship was very relaxed, probably due to the first rate instructors including Squadron Leader G. C. Kain, the B Flight O.C.

Our training was straight-forward bombing and gunnery practice, cross country both night and day, plus familiarisation with the aircraft. The seven weeks soon passed and on the 21st April we finished the course with a dinner and a night out in Chipping Norton with the rest of the course, plus instructors and a good time was had by all.

We left Moreton on the 22nd April (with rather heavy heads) for a few days' leave before reporting to 9 Bomber Squadron, based at Honington, Suffolk. It was arranged that the six of us should meet in Uxbridge Station Car Park and travel up to Honington in Vic Clarke's Buick; we needed the large car for six men with kit takes up a lot of space. It was late evening when we arrived at Honington, as our navigation had gone a little astray.

Reality was upon us; no more easy pleasant trips over friendly territory, this was the real thing.

The Sergeant's mess was deserted when we arrived, and the aircrew were sleeping five miles away in Ampton Hall; even so, one already felt the atmosphere and tension of an operational squadron, even if it was only to see the battle order (details of crews flying that night on operations) on the notice board.

The operation that night had been cancelled. It is hard to describe the atmosphere unless you were actually there.

We slept in the mess that night and were detailed to our quarters in Ampton Hall the following day after reporting to the Squadron Adjutant, who was at that time Flight Lieutenant Boothby, later Lord Boothby. I remember his booming but friendly voice very well. There was a slight change in the make up of the crews when arriving on the squadron. The senior pilot, in our case Vic Billett, was designated as co-pilot to another experienced crew, while their co-pilot was made our senior pilot and skipper.

How lucky our crew was in having Pilot Officer Keith Robinson of the Australian Air Force as our skipper and pilot; though only 20 years old, Keith was like an old hand, and in the months to come we would realise how his calm and cool approach at all times, especially in dangerous situations, was our salvation. No doubt he would say the same about his crew; perhaps his attitude rubbed off on us, in fact I know it did.

Due to the shortage of aircrew, there were nearly twice as many aircraft as crews, and the carrying of a co-pilot was a luxury, so as soon as B. G. Hawes had flown six operations, he was given his own crew and was then posted to a Middle East Squadron. The second pilot's position was not filled, so we were now a crew of five.

I can well remember the station commander Group Captain Dolly Gray flying as co-pilot, though whether he pumped the oil to the engines when required (this was a must in Wellingtons) I don't know.

I heard him asking our rear gunner, Jim Bell, whilst collecting his caffeine tablets (better known as "wakey wakey" tablets and supplied if required to reduce the risk of falling asleep), what they were for and on being told "to keep one awake" he quickly remarked, "I am too frightened to fall asleep."

On another occasion our Flight Commander Squadron Leader Cruickshanks asked the Flight Maintenance N.C.O. Flight Sergeant Styles to go as co-pilot, which he did; and he was quick to admit that he had not realised just how arduous and tiring as well as dangerous operations were. I met Flight Sergeant Styles three years later (now a Warrant Officer) and he still remembered the trip with pride.

As previously mentioned, though we had our meals in either the Officers' or Sergeants' mess, the sleeping quarters for aircrew were at

Ampton Hall, a large mansion set in its own grounds. It was a nuisance at times, mostly due to having to catch the coach to and from the airfield. The quiet and peaceful surroundings meant we always had a good night's or day's sleep, free from any air raids. We were five to six in a large room and the only piece of furniture was one bed each, no lockers or cupboards (very basic); but I never heard any grumbles: life was too short.

Our first two operational trips were what they called 'Make you learn', only to the French coast bombing the barges in the ports of Calais and Dieppe. To describe one's feelings before the first operation into enemy territory is not easy. Apprehensive, afraid of course (anyone without fear is dangerous), certainly butterflies in the stomach, wondering if we would come under enemy fire and if so, what our reaction would be. We did come under fire, not very intense, mostly tracer - nevertheless we were relieved to be on our way back and were soon to learn how different the defences were over Germany.

It was during this period that a valiant effort by the Station Commander Dolly Gray and the Medical Officer Squadron Leader McCarthy to save one of the squadron pilots from a blazing aircraft took place; they both received the award of the George Medal.

On the 15th May we at last appeared on the battle order for our first operation over Germany, the target being Hannover, a six to seven hour trip, which was a long time over enemy territory. This was followed by Kiel on the 18th, which would last the same time airborne but mostly over the sea.

To fly in bombers, especially at night, was an experience not to be found in any other command or service. There was a great contrast to sitting by the aircraft at dispersal on a sunny summer's evening with only the countryside sounds to be heard, relaxing and awaiting take-off. Suddenly, there would be a burst of engines starting up and preparing for departure, then taxying to the runway, receiving the green light from the Airfield Controller, and you were off: thundering down the runway with a maximum load and then airborne. Within an hour the enemy coast would be crossed and for the next five hours or more, intense concentration would be required awaiting expected attacks from fighters or being picked up by searchlights. The strain was unfortunately too much for some aircrew and they had to be taken off operations. This was described as L.M.F., Lack of Moral Fibre, which was absolute nonsense. I saw many colleagues suffer from this and it was not a lack of anything, it was a matter of whether one was built that way, or putting it in modern parlance, "thick skinned". We all have our breaking point, some sooner than others, and certainly no disgrace should be attached to this. Unfortunately the R.A.F. at that time did not seem to think so, but they had a lot to learn; it had to wait until aircrew who had had the experience were in control.

During this period our crew was selected with Squadron Leader Percy Pickard, well known later as "F" for Freddie in the film "Target for Tonight". He led the Mosquito attack on Amiens Prison releasing many resistance fighters, but sadly with the loss of his own life along with Flight Lieutenant Broadley (another ex 9 Squadron Colleague). The selection was for a painting of a Wellington Bomber and Crew by T. C. Dugdale A.C.A. This was a great honour and we were very thrilled. Mr Dugdale was later to become Vice Chairman of the Royal Academy. Later he showed deep understanding and sympathy to my parents when I was missing.

The Squadron was also visited by the Father of the Royal Air Force, Marshall The Viscount Trenchard. On landing he quickly broke up any formality, told us to gather round, and gave us words of praise and encouragement about how we were keeping up the morale of the country by hitting the enemy on his own soil. On the 27th May we were briefed to search in daylight for the Bismarck which had sunk the Hood and was heading for the French ports. While waiting to take off we were told the battleship had been sunk, but that we were to sweep the Channel towards Brest for one of the escorts, a Hipper Class Cruiser. It was a lovely sunny day as we flew down over Devon in formation to begin the search. The sweep was negative, and all returned to base after nine hours' flying. We lost an engine on the way back: the propeller fell off and the brakes failed on landing and we ended up on the far side of the airfield right on the edge of an old bomb crater. Operations continued over the next few nights, depending on the weather, which was not too friendly at that time, until 9th June. It was decided that four aircraft from 9 squadron should carry out a daylight sweep for enemy shipping off the French to Dutch coast. The crews selected were the Squadron Commander, Wing Commander Arnold, Squadron Leader Pickard, Flying Officer Lamb and ourselves. The sweep was not in formation as we had to make use of cloud cover. Due to a misunderstanding we found ourselves along the Dutch coast without any cloud cover and no sign of any of the other aircraft. We immediately hurried away from the coast and headed for home, not before dropping our bombs on an enemy convoy of ships. Our aircraft had hardly completed the bombing when we were attacked by an ME 109. The attack lasted nearly half an hour, with Jim Bell and myself who were in the rear and front turrets respectively managing to keep him at bay long enough for the enemy fighter to think about running out of fuel after which he was away back to his base, much to our relief.

Due to the long use of the guns, one in my turret overheated and exploded, filling the turret with black smoke: just as well we were on our way back to base. On arrival we later learned that only one other aircraft had returned, S/Ldr. Pickard's. After debriefing we had a meal and adjourned to Ampton Hall for a few jugs in the bar and to await any news of the other two. The next morning it was realised that there was no hope of the return of the other two, which meant that the squadron had lost its Commanding Officer along with the Navigation Bombing and Gunnery leaders. The whole squadron was stunned and a little shaken at this loss, especially of Wing Commander Arnold, who was to us all a real gentleman and one of the very few men whom I had great respect and admiration for; I would have followed him to the end of the earth. It was later learned that his crew were prisoners of war and they wrote a letter to the Squadron, describing their C.O.'s gallantry in allowing them to bale out at low altitude, while he kept the aircraft level. In so doing, Wing Commander Arnold left it too late to escape himself and perished when the aircraft crashed. Despite the great loss, the squadron continued operating. Many bombing missions were carried out for the rest of the month, sometimes two nights running; this was necessary to make a maximum effort. If it was announced that 80 to 100 aircraft were taking part in an operation, which raised a great cheer at briefing - far removed from the 900 to 1000 bombers in later years. Our crew continued operating during the next two months, apart from leave, which was approximately six days every six weeks. I should mention at this point that an extra leave allowance was given to all operational aircrew, thanks to the generosity of Lord Nuffield: little has been mentioned about this.

Visits to the Rhine Valley were very frequent, as this area was heavily defended. To reach the main part of Germany there was a twenty mile corridor where the concentration of searchlights and night fighters was extensive. We were caught in the search lights on several occasions and held for what seemed an age, which we were lucky to escape, apart from one when our hydraulics were hit by a night fighter; but we managed to get away, thanks to the magnificent airmanship of Keith Robinson and, of course, luck. To describe the feeling when caught by the searchlights is difficult: one is blinded by the beams and it gives the feeling of being caught naked in a crowd with nowhere to hide.

I recall an operation to Hamburg in the month of September when we saw three aircraft caught in the searchlights and shot down all in the space of five minutes. Our pilot was our original from training, Vic Billet. We were due to go on leave as soon as we got back as Vic was getting married and we had been invited. You can imagine how we felt when seeing this shooting down; the accuracy was unbelievable, so fingers were crossed for the rest of the mission, metaphorically anyway.

We were often hit by fighters and flak but our luck always held, plus, as previously mentioned, the adaptability of the Wellington.

There was one incident when, on an operation to the Rhine Valley, our rear gunner Jim Bell was hit between the eyes with a piece of shrapnel, so we had to drag him from the turret with blood everywhere. I took over his position while Vic Clarke tended to Jim's wound. He recovered quickly and was only missing from a few operations. Jim was reported missing two years later, something that happened so many times to one's colleagues. At the time we thought Jim was lucky not to lose an eye but I often wonder whether we were wrong, for at least he would not have been on operations and missing, with only one eye. I expect fate, whatever that is, has a lot to do with it.

When not on duty, our favourite place for having an enjoyable night out was Bury St. Edmunds. The most popular hostelry amongst our crew was The Suffolk Hotel in the Gentlemen Only Bar, supervised by Mabel, who kept us all in order, both civilian and service alike. Mabel may have appeared on the surface a bit of a crotchety soul, but underneath she had a heart of gold; many times we were allowed cigarettes hidden in the evening paper. This was a great honour as cigarettes were at a premium. Another hostelry of popularity was The Angel, famous for its mention by Mr Pickwick in

Charles Dickens' 'Pickwick Papers'; also Everards, but as far as we were concerned, the Suffolk was our base for a night off. There was one occasion when after returning from an operation on the 27th August it was reported that two of our crews had come down in the drink (sea), so after a quick snack we took off for a sweep along the coast and the North Sea with the remainder of the squadron.

This is only one example of the spirit and morale of the Squadron. Such were the acts of comradeship and recent successful raids that it was one of the most highly regarded squadrons in the Group. By the time we had landed and been briefed, had a wash and brush-up and such, it was not worth going to bed, so four of us went off to Bury for a visit to the Cinema. I decided for the one and only time to take the so called wakey wakey tablet, to keep me awake during the film. I remember taking my seat and it seemed as if only a minute had passed before my colleagues started nudging me to say the show was over and it was time to go and eat. I had slept during the whole show, so there were no more tablets for me.

Our pilot and skipper Keith Robinson completed his tour of operations towards the end of August and we were taken over by Squadron Leader Inness. I should point out that of our original crew, only Vic Clarke, Jim Bell and myself were still in the crew. Our first flight with the new skipper was to Mannheim on the 29th August. The flight out was no more eventful than usual until after dropping our bombs and turning for home, the pilot, while taking evasive action to avoid anti-aircraft, lost control of the aircraft which turned over on its back while at 12,000 feet.

The pilot regained control at 2000 feet, but owing to a misunderstanding, Vic Clarke and the navigator had left the falling aircraft. Despite losing many of the navigational instruments we managed to return to base using radio bearings.

This operation was the nearest to what I thought would be the last and the end of our time on this earth. There seemed to be no hope of recovery, being thrown about an aircraft, flying first on its back and then in a steep dive, to be followed by a roll which was most uncomfortable; one just hung on to anything available. Strangely, fear did not seem to come into it. Like the soldiers in the trenches in the First World War, the possibility of survival was remote, though you never thought it would happen to you. It is quite true that thoughts flash through your mind in a very quick time, naturally of the family at home (especially as my mother was just recovering from a serious operation), of special occasions and of people who have made an impression in your life.

A few days later after this operation I went on a week's course at Newmarket. We were billeted in a house in the town but ate in the mess, which was in one of the grandstands. There are two courses at Newmarket: one was still used for racing, where the Derby was held during the war years, and the other was occupied by the R.A.F. The waiters in the mess were ex-stablelads and it was always said that if you noticed a tear in their eyes while serving, there was probably one of their old charges on the menu.

I did have an unusual and sad experience during my short stay. At that time there was a hush hush squadron operating and their mission was to fly over and land in occupied territory, delivering agents and dropping supplies. Their aircraft were jet black Lysanders and Whitleys. We were therefore, on arrival, primed on security and the care we should take in whom we met or spoke to outside and in the town. On the very first night we went out, we were in the Golden Lion Hotel at the buffet bar when, what to me was a perfect stranger in civilian clothes, approached me, hand held out with, "Hello old chap, fancy seeing you again!" I expect from my hesitant handshake and expression, he realised I did not recognise him. My head was full of the security lectures and enemy agents. I can still see the look of disappointment in his face. The sad fact was he had been in a bad crash which disfigured his face and my not showing instant signs of recognition brought home to him the fact that he looked very different. He was, of course, a colleague of a past course I was on. However, after explaining our security brief etc. on enemy agents in the town plus a few beers, I think all was well; I hope so anyway. On returning to the Squadron, Jim Bell and myself joined a crew with our old pilot Vic Billet and finished our tour as part of his crew, with trips to Frankfurt, Hannover, Genoa (a long but easy trip) and Berlin, a long and arduous operation, with plenty of heavy defences and night fighters. The tour, 31 operations all told, finished on the 26th September and I spent the next few weeks in the flight offices; a little boring but I soon learnt the expression: "Do not volunteer".

I did break the rule once: one crew was short of a radio operator/front gunner, so to break the boredom I put my name down. The operation was cancelled that night but two days later we were down to go. However, during the break, one of the crew had returned from leave so my name was scratched out. The crew failed to return and were posted missing; no news was ever received as to their final outcome so the North Sea had most likely claimed them.

After six weeks on ground duty I was posted again to Newmarket on an updating radio course to last until the end of the year. I was stationed at Honington with 9 Squadron for nearly seven months and I can, without hesitation, say that they were one of the most efficient and looked upon as the most dependable of squadrons in Bomber Command; confirmation of this is in its record from inception to the present year flying the latest aircraft, Tornadoes.

During the period I was on the squadron we were lucky to have some of the finest airmen in the Royal Air Force. To name them would be an injustice to all who came before and after. The comradeship, unselfish attitudes and dedication was unsurpassed; and included of course are the gallant hard working ground crews who gave their full time and expertise in maintaining the aircraft and who were with us all the time on our trips and only relaxed on our return. I think our crew was one of the first crews to have a night out, both of air and ground crews, and what a time we had without thought of rank or duties!

I always felt, however, that the Station Headquarters Staff, apart from Station Commander and Medical Staff, never fully realised how serious and dangerous operations were or how small the survival rate was; they always seemed apart from the rest.

Two instances stand out in my mind:

1. Pay parades for the Squadron N.C.O.s were held every two weeks in the morning at 10.30. On one occasion we did not land till late and were not in bed until 06.00 (Ampton Hall 5 miles away) so we did not arrive back at camp until lunch time. As we were not on pay parade at the allotted time we would have to wait until the next day. Despite the intervention of the Squadron C.O., Adjutant etc., they would not change the routine. No thought was given as to whether we were short of cash and would be unable to enjoy a night off, maybe the last time for some. After this the time was changed to 15.30 hours, no doubt with pressure from the Station and Squadron Commander.

2. My request to be paid (I was going on leave) before operating one evening, so that I could go straight on leave after completing the operation, was turned down because, quote "you may be missing and

not return", a funny attitude considering I was already entitled to pay!

Attached to Honington at the time I was there was the Czechoslovakian bombing squadron. They operated from the satellite airfield but used our Mess and other facilities on a regular basis. They were a brave lot of lads, even if they appeared a little wild, when judged by our standards. We all got on well together and we always felt on our side a lot of sympathy for the Czechs having been taken over by the Germans.

There was a very amusing story that went the rounds, I think it was on a squadron of Wellingtons at Feltwell. The squadron had news that one if its missing aircraft had landed on an airfield in France in error and had been captured. This was of course hammered home to the squadron to see that no one fell into the Germans' trap again. A few weeks later one of the squadron aircraft landed at the Czech airfield, due to their own field being closed for bad visibility. They landed all right, and taxied to a point which they thought was correct. I should mention it was still dark. One of the Czech N.C.O.s, thinking it was one of his own squadron, opened the hatchdoor and shouted in Czech. The pilot of the British aircraft, not realising there was a Czech Squadron in England, straightaway thought of the previous episode and shouted, "Bloody hell! Germans!" restarted his engines, charged down the runway and took off, much to the annoyance of the air traffic staff. They landed safely at another airfield and felt very sheepish when told what had happened.

On the 15th November, I moved to Newmarket for the second time and had an interesting five weeks updating radio know-how. On completing the course and before being posted we were granted leave to cover Christmas and the New Year. Usually, when passing through London, I visited my elder sister in New Southgate and often stayed the night. On a few occasions there had been air raids in progress giving me an insight into what it was like to be on the receiving end, which was certainly frightening, even though the odds of surviving were much greater. I was always impressed by the kindness and respect shown to me while in London by the Londoners, especially transport personnel and taxi drivers. Many a free ride I had and I was plucked out of a queue by a taxi driver. I think there was a link or bond and maybe a little appreciation of what we were doing in hitting back at the enemy on his own doorstep.

On this particular leave I did stay with my sister and on getting up for breakfast and reading the morning papers, I found out that I had been awarded the Distinguished Flying Medal. Due to leaving the squadron and being on a course, the official announcement of the award was delayed and I was probably one of the very few who first saw it in the national papers.

It helped to make Christmas 1941 an enjoyable and relaxing leave.

CHAPTER 5

1942 - 43

After a very enjoyable leave, I returned to Newmarket on the last day of 1941 to be officially informed of my award. In the words of the then C.O. of 3 G.T. Flight-4 (Squadron Leader Stephens): "I understand you got a gong of some sort, jolly good show!" He was quite a character and had many interesting stories to tell. The only thing that annoyed him was that he was not allowed to join a squadron for operational flying (he was of course too old; around fifty-plus).

Our postings had arrived and I was on my way to 101 Squadron based at Oakington (the home of the famous future path finding 7 squadron). I was rather surprised that I was back on an operational squadron, as normally one had a rest after 30+ operations. I was soon informed, however, that the posting was an error and so I was on my way as an instructor to 11 Operational Training Unit at Bassingbourn in Hertfordshire. 11 O.T.U. was to be my posting for the next two years, a period of marking time, containing both uplifting and depressing times. In a way I was sorry to leave Oakington, having met many old friends and distinguished aircrew during my short stay. On arriving at Bassingbourn I was sent to Tempsford, a few miles away, as the concrete runways were being laid, putting the airfield out of commission. I was very lucky to meet up with two old pals from Moreton-in-Marsh, Sergeants Ralph Higham and Joe Mortimer, plus the then Flight Commander Squadron Leader Kain.

Being a temporary base was a bit disconcerting, as we were always ready to move when requested, so settling down was out of the question. Nevertheless it was an interesting and fairly quiet period to be introduced to the art of instructing and, as a small community, we got on well together. Very little of significance occurred during our stay. Visits to local hostelries in Tempsford and Sandy did not exactly set the place alight. The only amusing episode I can recall was when, having a drink in the local one evening, I noticed two well built girls drinking pints of ale (not usual in those days - most drank only halves). On remarking about this to my friend I was told they were the Vicar's girls. In my naïveté I instantly thought of the local Vicar and said what a shame his daughters drank like that, whereupon my friend laughed his head off: he explained that they were Vickers Armstrong girls who were repairing the fabric on the Wellingtons back at the airfield.

It was not long before Tempsford was required for operational requirements, so it was back to Bassingbourn, to use the airfield satellite Steeple Morden for flying only until the runways were completed, which was not to be until the month of May. It was during this period of travelling to Steeple Morden that, on returning one morning after an instructional flying exercise, the coach was involved in an accident with a railway van: it turned over on its back and threw us all over the place. Fortunately no one was seriously injured. The door was jammed but we managed to scramble out through the windows. The only damage I received was to my wrist watch: the front was knocked off and the face got cracked but it was still working. It is still working today, now in the possession of one of my helpers in Holland.

I went instructing in the afternoon and it was only on landing that I learned that all those involved in the crash were told to be off duty for the rest of the day. I must say I could have done with the rest as my head was aching and for the first time flying was not the cure. I was very lucky that my best cure for a hangover was always flying, and I am glad to say I never felt any ill effects from flying, physically anyway; mentally I am not so sure.

I should point out that I elected for flying instructing as I found (despite having parents who were both in the teaching profession) that classroom instruction was not my forte. When flying on instruction the aircraft always had an instructor pilot as well as a radio instructor: neither flew without the other. The instructor was to take the trainee crew on one day and one night cross country, which would incorporate practise bombing and gunnery. These trips usually lasted from four to five hours, which gave the crew a good insight into what was to be experienced (without of course encountering any opposition). This probably sounds like a soft option for the experienced aircrew, but unfortunately it was not like that at all. The aircraft used on O.T.U.s were those no longer needed on squadrons, so they were not up to operational standard; moreover they were being used day and night now for instruction. This resulted in the loss rate in training being on a high ratio, even with instructors, so it can be imagined what it must have been to new trainee crews with only a few hours' experience. I once saw the accident figures in training and found it staggering, even though on reflection at our own O.T.U. I was not surprised.

No blame can be attached to anyone as the demand for replacement aircrew was enormous. I would wish to point out that the ground crews worked like slaves to keep the aircraft flying. I had the highest admiration for these men. Always short of manpower, they worked long hours without much thanks (not like a squadron where each aircraft had its own crew). The state of the aircraft got to such a bad level that I myself had over 20 consecutive flights, which were very dodgy to say the least. It made one wonder whether it was safer on an operational squadron, though when seeing the squadron casualties, one realised this was not true.

The runways were at last finished, which meant flying direct from Bassingbourn, saving the time wasting and boring journeys to Steeple Morden.

In the middle of April, I was informed by the Adjutant that an investiture was to be held at Buckingham Palace on the 28th April at which I was to attend and receive the Distinguished Flying Medal from His Majesty King George VI. Two invitation tickets from the Lord Chamberlain were enclosed for two guests, which I sent home for my parents.

At the time, I had only one uniform, issued when joining up and constantly used, as Battle Dress was issued only a few months before. I was worried at its worn condition and pointed this out to the Station Adjutant, requesting permission to change it for a new one. This was quickly turned down, but I was told I could pay for a new one. This I did straight away and even had to pay a tailor in the nearby town, Royston, to fit it correctly. This usually meant alterations to the arms, mine being a little longer than the standard fit.

I travelled up to London on the 27th April and stayed the night with my sister. The following day I left my luggage at Waterloo station, then got a taxi to the Palace and joined a friend I knew to be there. We entered through the large gates and walked across the courtyard, then into the Palace. We went through the room for the investiture and into an ante-room where we were given a briefing on what to do; after that we lined up in the order of presentation. More than a hundred men and women were to be decorated that day and, as relatives and friends of the recipients were directed to their seats by members of the Home Guard, it was nice to see a good number of children present. The King, dressed in naval uniform, decorated the recipients from a small inclined platform, erected at the side of the gallery. An Army officer standing at the King's right hand called out the individual names of those entitled to an award. The latter approached His Majesty, turned smartly to the left to face the King, bowed and took two steps forward. After clipping the decoration on to the uniform or dress, His Majesty shook hands with the recipient and spoke a few words of congratulation and good wishes. In some cases he had a short chat and asked questions. The recipient then stepped back two paces, bowed and turning right, left the room by the opposite gangway.

An orchestra played the National Anthem at the beginning and at the end of the ceremony and throughout the presentation, light incidental music was played.

The investiture took about one hour and to me it was very impressive, being very informal without any of the red tape associated with many military occasions I have attended during and after the war.

I had to admit that despite the relaxed atmosphere, I felt quite nervous before the ceremony but quickly lost this, when seeing so many well-known heroes and heroines I had read about in the press.

On leaving the Palace we were quickly interviewed by the many reporters hanging around outside and then met up with my parents. We got the first train to Bournemouth, where I could spend the one extra day, before returning to Bassingbourn. I reflected on how right I was in deciding to buy a new uniform, for the rest of the recipients all looked very smart and were a credit to the occasion.

It was while on leave in late May that I received a recall and found that the O.T.U. was to take part in the first 1000 Bomber raid on Cologne. The O.T.U. formed crews from the instructors with the best aircraft for the highest rank, etc. I was crewed with Warrant Officer Mirfin, which meant we had the aircraft next to the last one, piloted by a Sergeant. After two days of waiting and preparation the raid took place on the 30th May. We had an uneventful flight to the target, though when arriving, it was an unbelievable sight: so many fires burning and even other aircraft could be seen. The only snag we had was that in a Wellington the oil had to be pumped to the engine and unfortunately we found our pump was useless, so whether the engines would hold out was the vital question.

While crossing the Dutch coast, one engine seized up and we lost the propeller and just afterwards the wireless generator blew up, leaving the radio useless. Not being able to use the radio I spent all my time trying to release the oil pump, hoping that at least the one remaining engine would survive. Unfortunately this did not happen and the pilot was soon warning us all to prepare for an emergency landing; at least we had by now crossed the Suffolk coast, which meant it would be a belly landing and not a ditching in the sea.

I braced myself against the main spar and waited while Jim Mirfin, the pilot, kept us informed about what he was doing; with a piece of magnificent airmanship he brought the aircraft in on to a field, grazing and clipping the tops of the surrounding trees, and made a perfect belly landing. We stopped in a short distance, the smell of ploughed up earth penetrating the aircraft, as well as the earth itself, coming in through the floor. I was thrown to one side on impact and felt a wet substance trickling down my face. At once I thought I must have cut myself and was bleeding, but on further investigation I found it was oil which had burst out of the wretched pump I had been working on; it had freed itself and was now working all right.

After a short silence we confirmed over the intercom that all the crew were O.K. and then clambered out through the emergency exits. Being a short night, the dawn was already breaking and Jim Mirfin and Taffy Jones, the navigator, decided to seek help and the use of a phone. They apparently had difficulty at first as the occupants of the nearest houses were reluctant to answer the door for fear they were Germans who had crashed. It was not long before they were able to contact base who got in touch with a small Army camp which was guarding radar masts and some sort of communications. The latter quickly sent transport to pick us up, in fact their officer commanding came with the transport and took us back to their camp. There were only 3 or 4 officers in the camp and they soon invited us (despite being either Warrant Officers or N.C.O.s) into their mess, firstly for a beer; this was the first time I had drunk a beer so early in the day, round about 5 a.m.!

We then had an excellent breakfast, at the same time recounting our trip and the first time raid with 1,000 bombers. Afterwards we awaited transport back to Bassingbourn.

The Commanding Officer sent his own transport and soon we were on our way having received the usual first class treatment from the Army. I always experienced this type of welcome when visiting Army camps, either socially or on duty. Their hospitality was extraordinary and I understand that this was widespread among the different services. The only pity was that it did not percolate to the top brass, where jealousy and envy was far too much in evidence, according to reports. I shall return to this subject in my summing-up.

We were soon back at Bassingbourn, eager to hear the news and whether there were any other casualties. We had only lost one aircraft, the one after ours, yes indeed the oldest one, flown by an all sergeant crew. My friend Ralph Higham was in this aircraft but thankfully, at a later date, we learnt they were still alive and all of them were prisoners of war.

We missed the next 1,000 bomber raid as no aircraft was available; apparently it was not a success due to the weather which had been perfect for the Cologne raid, just as well as far as we were concerned.

Training went on during the next two months, along with air tests for further 1000 raids, which never materialised, due to shortage of serviceable aircraft among the training units. It was not until early September that a further raid took place (not a 1000 bomber), this time to Düsseldorf, which was again unsuccessful owing to the poor weather. Our trip was uneventful and we resumed training again without any further operations.

There was one amusing occurrence during this period which perhaps confirmed the difference in attitude and discipline between the Army and the Air Force, which is only natural when looking at the make-up and functioning of the different services; and I certainly do not intend to decry the Army by relating the incident. When taking trainee crews on a cross country exercise we often carried an Army officer (who were seconded to the unit for a week or more for flying experience) with us. On this particular afternoon I was walking to the aircraft to prepare for the trip when I passed an Army captain who hailed me in a tone of superiority as follows: "Sergeant, are you going on this flight? If so, carry my parachute to the aircraft!" I looked at him in amazement. Fortunately the pilot instructor on the trip, who happened to be the Flight Commander, was approaching. I called over to him and explained the Army officer's request. I will not repeat the language the pilot used on him but in no uncertain terms he explained that, firstly, you always carried your own gear on to a flight, and secondly, aircrew instructors of whatever rank are not servants. At this the officer apologised and picked up his parachute, but unfortunately by the release handle, thus opening up the chute all over the place. This was too much for our Commander who proceeded to give him a lecture on airmanship. In the meantime I could see how embarrassed the officer was, so I quickly gathered up the open chute, telling him that for half a crown (this was the payment for the W.A.A.F.s who packed the chutes) I would change it for him.

I returned with a new one and on the exercise I was able to explain that in the Air Force, crews were mostly working as one, and rank did not apply when flying; at least I always found this to be so.

We had heard rumours that we were to move to another complex to make way for the American Air Force and soon this was to become reality when news came that we would have to leave for Westcott, west of Aylesbury. The explanation given was that where we were going the facilities were well dispersed and as we did a lot of night flying it was safer this way. Bassingbourn was a permanent airfield where all the buildings were close together and in the event of bombing, casualties would be heavy when there was night flying. This was the story we were given. We were not too keen to leave our warm comfortable quarters and crew rooms, all conveniently arranged, in exchange for cold Nissen huts, some over half a mile from the Mess. There was no hot water unless you walked a quarter of a mile to the ablutions; moreover there was an even longer walk to the crew room and the offices. Bicycles would be supplied, as we were told, but we never saw any, probably because they were commandeered by the Station Headquarter's Staff.

I was lucky managing to purchase one for a pound from one of the trainees on his posting to a conversion unit. Strangely I never heard many grumbles; probably everyone, like myself, thought it was part of the war effort and maybe it stood us in good stead for the future, as actually it would turn out that way in later experiences.

We were fortunate at 11 O.T.U. to have a great instructing staff. We were all fairly experienced and were able to pass on any expertise we knew to the trainees passing through. As most of us had done over 30 trips it was a great encouragement for them to know it was possible to survive, even if the average rate was between 5 and 10 trips, depending on the time of year and location.

I had happy memories of Bassingbourn with the visits to the local hostelries and to Royston to have a meal at the local café, which was unfortunately in the wars with the Ministry of Food by selling steaks without mentioning they were horse steaks. I remember with amusement hearing one of many Australian aircrew declaring that he did not care what the steaks were, as they had tasted delicious - "But I shall never go there again," he added.

Our favourite inn was The Hoops in the village of Bassingbourn, with Ma Baker presiding. She was a great character and looked after us well; in the end she was sorry to see us leave. Many a farewell party was held at her establishment late into the night on special occasions. I am sure she also got on well with the Yanks when they arrived.

The only other memory which brings a smile to my face is that during our last three months, we slept in a large house a mile down the road from the airfield, a place called Kneesworth. No transport was supplied, so a walk every morning and evening was necessary, for no public transport was available either. At that time hundreds of Italian prisoners of war were working on the land and they were supplied with transport to take them to their destination. We used to wave as they passed us, trudging along the road to camp, especially in the rain. We often wondered about them but they always seemed to see the funny side.

We soon settled down at Westcott and the business of training continued with very little delay. I was not able to get home for Christmas in 1942, so saw the New Year 1943 in at a mess party.

1943 was, for the most part, an uneventful year for me, at least until near the end. Apart from many near misses due to the aircraft (as previously mentioned) being old, the few outstanding memories were away from flying and more of an off-duty nature. I made my main base for off duty leisure at the small village of Ashenden up on the hill, overlooking the airfield. I got to know nearly all the inhabitants and they were the most kind and friendly people I have met. They made me feel at home and I can truthfully say that thanks to their generous nature I was able to relax and enjoy many an hour forgetting the war. They even got a cricket eleven together and challenged the camp team (of which I was a member) to two matches.

We played on the ground in Waddesden Manor, owned by the Rothschilds. Much fun and enjoyment was gained from these matches and strangely enough we lost both, which added to the leg-pulling on both sides, while enjoying a pint or two.

Another unusual experience I had was whilst on duty one evening in the watch tower. There was an all ranks dance on in one of the hangars and suddenly a call came through for the ambulance (or blood wagon as we called it) to go to the hangar at once. It was around midnight and no flying from our field was taking place, so I jumped in with the duty crew and raced to the hangar to find that one of the young airwomen had gone hysterical (probably had a little too much to drink) and was running around naked, screaming her head off.

We grabbed some blankets and it was unbelievable the difficulty we had in getting hold of the girl, wrapping her in blankets and getting her to the sick-bay. It was hard to describe; in fact it was horrible to see a person in such a state and she was like a slippery eel. The next morning everyone was remarking, "Lucky old Blakey, trust him to get the best job," but it was not like that. To see a pretty girl unclothed may be nice but not in these circumstances and we had only one thought: to get her safely to a place where she could be treated.

Instructing continued, training more aircrew to face very little hope of survival. It reminded me a little of the action of "going over the top" in the First World War: very little hope but no sign of despair, a job had to be done, giving hope to all at home and to those in the occupied countries.

The instructors were gradually being called back to the squadrons and many pilots said they would call for me to join them, but eventually they had little say in what crews they could form and I regret that in most cases they failed to survive, so my luck held out.

I was very fortunate in making friends with a son of one of the local farmers and they were very good to me, for on many occasions I was loaned a gun and their dog, so I could wander over the fields and through the woods, looking for game; not that I ever saw much or had many shots. The sheer joy of relaxing, thus getting away from the strains of flying and all that it entailed, was hard to describe but I can, without hesitation, say it was a welcome break. The countryside around Westcott was some of the best parts of Buckinghamshire, not too flat and yet satisfactory for flying, except for one hill south of the airfield which sadly was the end of several crews during my period of instructing there.

As previously mentioned, the experienced instructors were gradually being recalled to the squadrons and it was in the month of November that I was informed that I would be attached to one of the trainee crews coming through. I was not too happy about this as I had always been used to flying with experienced pilots.

I got no satisfaction from Group Headquarters as to why this was happening to me, so I wrote to a friend at Bomber Command, who regretfully informed me that by spreading experienced aircrew in new crews it not only boosted their morale, but made the odds of some aircrew surviving two tours of operation greater. I accepted this and joined my new crew to go through the O.T.U. course. I was around this period informed that I had been accepted for a commission and was waiting for it to come through. It seemed strange following the course through but I found it was at least a change, and the crew I was attached to were all N.C.O.s who were a credit to the various Royal Air Forces. They were very keen and I felt like a father looking after his children. I was so much older, not in age but in experience, and they all looked to me for advice and help. It was a nice feeling and it made the course and time go by more easily.

We celebrated Christmas on the camp knowing that we only had to carry out a leaflet raid to complete our training, which was to be on the 29th December. The leaflet raid was to Paris, no doubt part of the preparation for the invasion in six months' time. The trip was uneventful though remembering my own first trip way back in 1941, I could imagine how the rest of the crew felt. We did have some trouble with the photo flash, due to the bomb aimer's negligence, which resulted in his removal from our crew. This did not prevent us from celebrating the New Year and we all wondered what 1944 would bring; would this be the year of Victory or was the war to linger on, though all the signs pointed to a big push sometime in the near future?

CHAPTER 6

1944

On completion of the course we went on leave prior to a posting on "Battle Course" at Methwold in Suffolk. The Battle Course was a "toughening up" and "get fit" exercise along with training, in case of landing in enemy-held territory. How useful this turned out to be in the future! I certainly needed some physical training, as the last had been at Morecambe way back in 1940, and I did feel the benefit, although it was tough going and hard work.

The one most useful exercise was when we were taken out several miles from the camp at night, dropped without any aids, apart from one map, and then had to find our way back to camp without being detected. The Army, Home Guard and other units were on exercise to find us. The first action we took was to find a public phone box, which of course had no exchange in it, and ask the operator for a trunk call. While getting the number we required, she had to give her exchange to the one she was calling. As soon as we heard the exchange we rang off and though we might be several miles away from the exchange, at least we knew now to which area we had been dropped.

The crew split out into two's and off we went. Actually, it was not too bad; the only difficulty was that when making across country the area was full of wide deep dykes, owing to the drainage systems, devised by our friends from Holland in the past. Little did I realise that I would be seeing drainage systems on a much larger scale in the next few months.

During the Battle Course my commission came through so I had to go on leave to get fixed up with my new uniforms etc., which made a nice break. I was soon fixed up with the necessary equipment and returned after a few days to enjoy the delights of being a member of the Officers Mess. I had never realised what a difference in accommodation and food there was. I had always had a good appetite during my career and at several postings had found the food inadequate, so I had spent a lot of my pay on eating food outside. The food was very basic in the Sergeants Mess. (This was not the case at some camps where the caterers took an interest and the food was not disappearing on the black market.) After the main meal at midday there was only high tea and probably a bowl of soup for supper or even left-overs from tea. We were unfortunate in the Sergeants Mess for there was no other facility for eating, unlike the other ranks up to Corporal, who had the N.A.A.F.1, or the officers, who not only had lunch (like the main meal in the Sergeants Mess) but a full dinner at night as well. I can truthfully say that I did not have to eat out again, unless I did so at my own desire, which I eventually did from another squadron.

At the end of the course we were posted to Stradishall, a few miles away, for conversion on to Stirlings. This was certainly an interesting aircraft and very roomy, but their main use was the towing of gliders; even so, some were still operating over Germany.

We used to have one afternoon off a week, so I took the opportunity to cycle over to Halstead in Essex, about 12 miles or more away, to see my sister Dorothy and her young family. My brother-in-law Alf was with the Army overseas. On the journey I used to pass United States Army Air Force Bases and several times saw them returning from operations very badly hit. They certainly had a tough time and it was not surprising their casualties were high, especially in the beginning. It was very sad, as they were wonderful hosts, and their treatment if you had to land at their base was unforgettable. Although we may have pulled each others' legs on many occasions, the admiration and respect on both sides, especially amongst the active aircrew, was of the highest order.

The one amusing episode when at Stradishall was on arriving when we had to report to the Administration Officer who was a young Squadron Leader pilot, full of bounce and sarcastic comments. As usual, I was very quiet and said very little; I was wearing my raincoat at the time, so hiding my medal ribbons. This young squadron leader was soon giving us a lecture on what an easy time we had had so far but that we now had to face up to reality and that we were only still wet behind the ears, including many other cynical remarks. I was amazed at this as I would have thought the opposite approach necessary. He was not satisfied and seeing that I was the only officer in the crew made some comments regarding my having to obtain guts and stamina, etc. I was extremely disgusted with his attitude and just stared at him, thinking it would be best to ignore him. Later that evening, while having a drink in the Mess, the Squadron Leader came to the bar, looked at me, saw my ribbons and went red in the face. However, he instantly came over, apologised for his attitude earlier and bought me a drink. This was fine up to a point, but I wondered what happened to other aircrew who were not experienced like myself and would have taken his words seriously. It always seemed strange to me that there were very rarely men of the right experience, knowledge and understanding in positions where attitudes and treatment of aircrew were so important.

The course at Stradishall lasted just under 6 weeks and we were then posted to Syerston near Newark for further conversion flying on Lancasters for 4 weeks.

The course was uneventful apart from two incidents, one serious and the other I expect one could say amusing. The first incident was while walking back to the Mess one afternoon, after completing our flying programme. I happened to look up at one of the Lancasters flying near the airfield and, to my horror, the aircraft, which was flying straight and level, suddenly lost one of its wings; it seemed to break off and naturally the plane nose dived to the ground which resulted in a loud bang and the tell-tale pall of smoke rising from behind some trees. A message was broadcasted for anyone having witnessed this accident to report to Headquarters. I did so and it appeared very few people had seen it. All I was told was not to talk or discuss it with anyone. This seemed very strange to me as it was quite normal to discuss any accident and to hear why it had occurred. I never heard any more about this case, though I must say I was posted, or rather, we were posted, to 619 Squadron at Dunholme Lodge in Lincolnshire.

Dunholme Lodge, being a war time station, was well dispersed; in fact the area where I had my living quarters was just off the village near the parish church. My stay there was less than 3 weeks long, owing to the unfortunate loss of our pilot. The practice apparently was to let the pilot of new crews fly as second pilot on one or two trips, before taking their own crew on operations. Our pilot regretfully did not return from his first trip (he was taken prisoner and returned to New Zealand after the war), so the rest of the crew, including myself, were spare bodies.

After a few days, the rest of the crew were slotted in with other crews while I was posted to 52 Base at Scampton (original home of 61 Dambusters squadron) where I spent two pleasant weeks, awaiting a further posting.

Just before I left Dunholme Lodge I was lucky to meet in the local pub Warrant Officer Styles (previously mentioned during my 9 Squadron service).

My stay at Scampton was short and very relaxing, in fact all I was waiting for was a crew, so I was able to investigate Lincoln at my leisure. For the first time for many years I could sit back and enjoy a few days' rest away from the bustle of flying, which was no longer my favourite pastime. I think the experiences at 11 O.T.U. had taken the pleasure and enjoyment out of flying for me. I had always been so keen on getting in the air that I volunteered for any trip (other than operations) and the longer I was in the air the better I liked it. It was different now, maybe I was getting tired like many other aircrew. The strain and the odds of not surviving getting shorter and shorter were beginning to tell; but make no mistake, the dedication and eagerness to finish the war were still very strong, especially with the success of the Russians and the Allies in Italy and the beginning of the last chapters of World War II was in sight.

My posting to a new crew eventually arrived and once again I found myself at Syerston to meet the new crew and get a few days' flying in. We were all experienced aircrew, either starting a second tour or halfway through the first. The crew was as follows:

- Pilot: Squadron Leader King Cole DFC
- Navigator: Flight Lieutenant Jack Craven DFC
- Radio: Flying Officer Eric Blakemore DFM
- Bomb Aimer: Flight Sergeant Beresford
- Engineer: Flight Sergeant Ken Ingram
- Upper Turret: Flight Sergeant Fred Shorter
- Rear Turret: Sergeant Paul Hayes.

We soon finished our short training course and went on our way to 50 Squadron stationed at Skellingthorpe on the outskirts of Lincoln. Skellingthorpe was a well dispersed airfield and 50 Squadron shared it with 61, which meant it was rather crowded.

Our sleeping quarters were on the opposite side to the mess so it was either cycle, catch any transport going to the other side or walk, which was an impossibility due to the distance.

The sleeping quarters were in a Nissen hut accommodating about

10 officers. There were no proper washing facilities and everything was very primitive, to say the least. As it was summer the conditions were tolerable especially as I was promised a single room within the next few weeks. I was very surprised to learn many years later that the hostels built to accommodate factory workers had either single or double rooms with hot and cold water, either in the rooms or under the same roof: what a far cry from the facilities previously mentioned. I often wonder whether the people that were responsible ever gave it any thought or just looked upon aircrew (or come to that upon all other personnel) as merely people in uniform who would not dare to grumble or go on strike; which was no doubt different from some of the militant workers, who would down tools at the slightest pretext. Well, I expect they were right as I certainly heard many complaints about food but very few about living accommodation.

A few days after our arrival on 50 Squadron we were given a few days' leave, which happened to be just before "D-day", which was the reason why many trains were cancelled, so it took me nearly 24 hours to get from Lincoln to Bournemouth. The worst part was from Grantham to London for I had to wait almost eight hours at Grantham for a train. It was a very hot day and I retreated to a cinema where at least it was cool and I saw two performances to while away the time.

It was obvious that the invasion of Europe was imminent and that the big push would be on at last. The announcement of the Invasion was made while I was on leave and even though the weather was not up to what was required, there was much relief on learning that they had been fairly successful in most areas.

I returned from leave just after "D-day" and soon settled into the routine normally found on a squadron. As our pilot was the Flight Commander and Jack Craven was Flight Navigational Officer they had a choice as to which operations we should take part in. We did two sorties to France on the 10th and 14th June and a few days later we were all put on stand-by for what was described as "the big one". This apparently was to be a 2000 Bomber raid in daylight by both the Royal and United States Air Forces, accompanied by 2000 fighters on Berlin.

Jack Craven was engaged that evening in organising the routes etc., so I went into Lincoln on my own. The town was deserted due to the moving out of the United States Army to France etc. It was unbelievable to see so many girls wandering around the town, looking for something to do now that their boyfriends had gone. I had a few drinks with my old crew from Dunholme Lodge and then retired to bed, to be woken at 4 a.m. by a broadcast on the tannoy that operations were cancelled.

I did not see Jack until lunch time the next day as he had been up late into the night on the now cancelled operation. King Cole, our pilot, decided that (even though Jack let him know it was a trip to the Ruhr) we should take part in the night's operation, so we all went on a test of the aircraft we were to use that night and after that our briefing, where we learnt it was to be the oil refineries at Scholven Buer. The weather was fine that afternoon and evening and we were all in good heart when making our way to the aircraft Lancaster 11 840 "M" ready for take-off on the shortest night of the year, i.e. 21st of June.

Little did we know that this was to be our last operation and that we would be away from home for many months; in the case of 3 members of the crew, they were never to return.

The trip out was fairly normal: there seemed to be a lot of activity by enemy fighters, at least from the information provided by our radar. The forecast for the target area was to be clear all night but unfortunately, like most of the weather forecasts even today, they were way out for all we had was 10/10 cloud tops 3000 feet, no moon; but come midsummer night the moonless sky was bright making our aircraft easy targets for the enemy fighters. We arrived over the target without any mishaps; intense flak was met, accurately predicted up to 18/20000 feet; we carried out our mission and headed for home. Everything went well for the first 15 minutes, when all of a sudden there was a loud bang in one of the starboard engines and it began to race away, making a terrible sound and leaving a trail of exhaust flame. We realised that we had been hit by a fighter and the pilot informed us that he was having difficulty with the controls.

Unfortunately at the moment we were hit, our Rear Gunner, who had already had a previous bad experience, bailed out; at least John Lane reported the turret was empty. After about 10 minutes our pilot Tim Cole let us know that he was unable to keep the aircraft under control and that we were losing height, so we would have to bale out. We all prepared ourselves for the operation and left by the front escape hatch - first the bomb aimer, then the flight engineer, followed by navigator Jack Craven and myself. I imagined that the pilot left just after us and that the other two got away from the rear escape hatch, but unfortunately this turned out to be incorrect. When the aircraft eventually hit the ground and burst into flames Warrant Officer John Lane and Flight Sergeant Shorter were found to be still in the aircraft and were killed on impact. They were later buried in Holland at Epe cemetery, where I was many years later able to pay my homage.

To jump out of an aircraft for the very first time is, as anyone who has done it knows, something unknown in any sphere. There is a feeling of apprehension, fear up to a point, and the urge to do the jump (maybe the same feeling as knocking on the dentist's door: could it not be put off till later?). Fortunately for me there was none of this; when you know that if you don't go it will mean death or serious injury, there is no holding back. So out I went after the other three, counted ten, pulled the rip cord and suddenly after falling in space (the same feeling as in a dream), with a slight jerk I was sitting comfortably looking down into the dark, dropping at a slow speed and I must admit it was a very pleasant feeling.

Being midsummer the night was not totally dark and I could see that I would be landing in open fields with no trees (there was very little wind to speak of). It was difficult to estimate the actual height, but remembering all the instructions of previous courses, I bent my knees and landed fairly comfortably on the grass.

What were my thoughts as I descended by parachute, which in time was hard to judge, but certainly took 3 or 4 minutes? Apart from watching and attempting to focus on what I was to land in or on, the obvious thought straight away was that after over 40 operations, fate had at last caught up with me and that my time had finally come. However, I could be thankful that first, I had managed to survive so long; second, I was still alive and so far uninjured; and third, being so near the Dutch border the odds of escaping would be greater as long as I kept out of the enemy's hands.

It was during my descent that the aircraft crashed, burst into flames and even though it was a fair distance away, the explosion of ammunition and petrol tanks could be easily heard. With the aircraft crashing away from where I landed, this would at least give me some time to get away from the area.

I quickly released my parachute, gathered it up (and what a bundle it was with the harness and chute!) and then found myself surrounded by a herd of young cattle, all very interested in the object that had just landed from the sky. I had to shoo them away so that I could walk to the edge of the field in order to bury the equipment. I noticed that there was someone else from the plane in the next field, so after covering up the harness and chute, I probed my way through the fence to find Jack Craven, carrying out his burying routine. We shook hands and congratulated each other on still being in one piece after which we sat down in the field for a while before deciding on our next move.

Jack had a rough idea that we should be just on the Dutch/German border, so with a compass which I always carried, we set off towards the South. We made our way across fields and along a farm track to where we came across our first farmhouse. It was already beginning to get light and as we saw some movement around the farm buildings, we crept up to see an elderly man making his way to, we guessed, milking the cows. We quietly called to him and explained by signs who we were, to which he looked very frightened (which was only natural as we might have been Germans posing as R.A.F. aircrew) and we knew by his reaction that he wanted to get away from us. Nevertheless we managed with the help of one of the escape maps to get him to show us where we were and also he warned us as to where the Germans were stationed in the town of Epe. The actual spot where Jack and I had landed was about 3 miles away from the place where the aircraft crashed, which was Oene. We decided to walk away from the direction of Epe and as it was now very light we made our way to a cereal field which had the crop up to 4 feet high. We crawled to the centre and settled down to await the next night, some 18 hours ahead; a long wait but at last a chance to have some sleep and rest. Before each operation on a squadron every member of aircrew collected a small amount of foreign currency, applicable to the territory he would be flying over, and also an emergency ration pack. These were handed back on returning after the operation. It was an automatic procedure, just collecting the two packs and putting them in the best available pocket or whatever other place was convenient. I do not remember ever inspecting them, even though they were never the same packs.

Before every operation I always saw that my cigarette case was full and that I had my lighter, thus ensuring that I would have a good supply of cigarettes to smoke or share in an emergency. As Jack had been on late duty the night before, his supply was limited, but nevertheless was enough combined to keep us going in steadying our nerves or whatever they were supposed to do!

We then inspected our emergency ration packs; this was the first time I had actually looked into one, and what did we find? All the edible rations were mouldy, so quite useless, and even the tablets for converting water for drinking looked suspect, so that was that. We wondered how often these packs were inspected back at base, or were they just taken in and out week, month and year after year?

I forgot to mention that we were always issued with a small pack of rations to use on the flight. Firstly, a flask of fresh coffee if wanted (I never bothered for my flask back in the early days always got dropped and made useless), plus a bar of chocolate, a packet of chewing gum and some barley sugars. Jack and I still had these so we did not go without during our long wait. Thank goodness the weather was fine and sunny.

All during that wait we heard very little: voices in the distance and two aircraft flying in the vicinity, otherwise everything seemed peaceful and quiet. We were thankful for a long sleep and rest, even if it was on the ground.

At last, night began to fall and as soon as it was dark we headed across the fields to find a road that ran beside a canal, which would lead us south towards the town of Vaassen.

Everywhere was very quiet, owing to the curfew, except for the continuous croaking of frogs, which came from the canal. We crossed and recrossed one or two canal bridges to see if we were on the right track, but unfortunately the self-operated swing bridges were made of iron, making silent walking very difficult.

We were both now feeling rather famished and Jack started to suffer from severe stomach pains which made further progress out of the question. We decided to seek help as soon as it was light at the most isolated farm we could find. We were in luck for surveying a seemingly safe place, we also saw the farmer approaching us on his own, away from the house, evidently starting his rounds early. We need not have worried; although we knew that the vast majority of Dutch people would be very willing to help, there was always a chance of meeting the odd one who was either afraid or a traitor. In this case, however, after making conversation by the odd word and signs, we were invited into the house, where we met the farmer's wife who quickly prepared for us a hot drink and food.

House in Apeldoorn where the de Vries' lived and hid Jack and myself

(Top) Christen family in Barnweldt

(Bottom) 1942

(Top)   *1944*

*(Bottom,
left to right)*   *Crew, March 1944.
Nav., Bomb Aimer, Author
Mid Upper Gunner
Engineer, Pilot, Rear Gunner*

(Top)   Visiting the grave of F/Sgt. Ingram, crew member murdered by Gestapo Oct. 1944

(Bottom)   Meeting Dutch helpers Bob and Daisy de Vries (left)

Our first helper told us that he would contact the Resistance Movement in the area, who would then decide what we should do. In a very short space of time two men were introduced to us who spoke fair English and explained that they would make arrangements for us to be moved to a safe house and that a Police Inspector would pick us up in a car and take us to Apeldoorn, south of Vaassen. Meanwhile they questioned us (not regarding our service career) as regards many things so that they could be sure we were not a plant, even though they knew some R.A.F. men had bailed out and were somewhere in the district.

As the pick up would not arrive until the afternoon we had plenty of time to communicate with our new friends, mostly by Jack doing some sketches to explain what he was talking about. In the meantime I fell asleep and woke up just in time to enjoy a good Dutch farmhouse meal, very welcome in the circumstances, for I had to admit that I was as usual very hungry. Jack was still suffering from his stomach pains so he was unable to appreciate the meal.

At about 3 o'clock in the afternoon the Police Inspector arrived in a police car and after giving us the once over explained he was to take us to the Police barracks (station) in the town of Apeldoorn. We both stepped into the back of the car and were quickly driven off down the road at high speed, meanwhile keeping well out of sight, so that no one could wonder who we were, although no doubt we looked no different to other criminals of a different kind!

We naturally found the journey interesting and apart from the odd enemy soldier here and there, everything looked as normal as it would do back home.

We at last reached the Police barracks and the Inspector showed us where the Germans were billeted and their eating mess. (They were all out on duty, so there was no risk.) Then he told us to take off our uniforms and change into civilian suits which he had produced, as this would not make us so obvious.

After changing we were taken to the home of a schoolmaster who would put us up for one night, while other arrangements were made. We were very well looked after and it was quite a treat to be able to have a bath and sleep in a bed again which we were ready for; it meant the end of a very long day for us.

The next day, the 24th of June, we were introduced to the famous Dutch omelette for breakfast after which we stayed with the schoolmaster until the afternoon, when we were escorted by a young policeman to his house as a temporary move. His wife and child were away for the evening and we spent a pleasant few hours with him until further Resistance members arrived with bicycles to make the next move to a permanent safe house.

It seemed very strange cycling through a town occupied by the enemy, seeing German soldiers out for the evening, strolling around the cafés and shops. The time was around 9 p.m. (2100), so most people were on the move as the curfew was 10 p.m. (2200). Eventually we arrived at a large house, surrounded by a fair sized garden, where we were quickly ushered in the back door and up a staircase to a bedroom; there we met the senior member of the family who were to hide and protect us for the next 3 months or more. Mr. de Vries explained that there was a party downstairs to celebrate his daughter's final examination results and that as soon as everyone had gone home we could come downstairs.

This was of course the reason why we had heard the sound of dance music and voices of young people enjoying a party, which at first had surprised Jack and myself probably due to the last 48 hours experience; anyway it was nice to hear that all was not doom and gloom and it helped to raise our spirits.

We were rather taken aback though when Mr. de Vries also informed us that there was a German woman billeted in the house so we would have to be careful that she did not see us.

Within a short while the party was over and all the guests had gone home, so we were invited to go downstairs and meet the rest of the family. Mr. de Vries introduced Jack and myself to Mrs. de Vries, his wife, Bob his son and his daughter Nancy for whom the party was held. The whole family was very keen to hear our news, both of ourselves and the progress of the war, during which we were once again well fed and also had a slightly stronger drink to celebrate our arrival. Even at this early stage we could feel the eagerness and kindness the Dutch people showed in wanting to help and do their bit towards bringing about the downfall of the enemy. It was all very heartening and helped to alleviate the disappointment in our sudden departure from doing the same.

After a long exchange of news and information, interspersed with Jack's humour (Jack was a Yorkshire detective in civilian life so had a good gift of the gab and could tell a good story, both humorous and serious), we were taken to our very comfortable room, where we were soon hitting the hay. Thus our stay at Frisolaan 5 in Apeldoorn had begun and this was to last until that fateful Saturday September 30th, 1944.

We soon settled down in our new home, thanks to the wonderful welcome and treatment at the hands of our hosts. We were exceedingly lucky to have found such a safe house as this; Mr. de Vries had invented some extra safe hide-outs for us. In case some Germans might search the house for young men (unwilling to work for the Germans), we would quickly be put away in an upstairs shoes' closet; these were arranged all along the shelves, and beneath the middle shelf at the back of the closet the wall was not a real wall, but a piece of cardboard painted as such, which could be removed in order to give at least a temporary hiding place for two men crouching. This closet seemed so crammed with shoes that no one would expect a hiding place behind it.

Downstairs in the living room was a bigger place to hide; also a kind of closet with shelves, where the two of us could easily stand or sit down. This one was only meant for hide-out in case some neighbour or friend of the family would pop in while we were in the downstairs region and would have no time to hide upstairs in our own room.

Over the next 3 months we were better fed than we would have been at home, which proved of great importance during the last 6 months of evading when the supplies of food got less and less.

Our host Mr. de Vries had a chocolate and manufacturing business in Vaassen, about 7 miles North of Apeldoorn, which was still partly functioning, so during the week he and his son Bob were away at work while Mrs. de Vries and Nancy looked after Jack and myself.

The German woman, Frau Bohres, who was billeted in the house (much to the annoyance of the whole family·de Vries), was the mother of the secretary to the "Reichskommissar", i.e. Governor General of Holland, the highest ranking official in this occupied country.

As this so-called "Reichskommissariat" also used to sign the death warrants of Dutch people opposing the Nazis, one can understand that these German women entering Frisolaan 5 at the time were met in an icy cold atmosphere.

The Frisolaan house was the safest in Holland, for no German would dare to ask questions or start searching the premises while that secretary and her mother were living there. "Old Frowzy" (as Jack and I used to call her) had a room upstairs and her daughter, "Young Frowzy", had a smaller living room downstairs at her disposal, the room next to the big room where we, the Dutch and English, used to be.

As long as we could keep out of Frowzy's way there was nothing to worry about. The daughter had her work of course, so she was not very often in the house, but her mother had a nasty habit of coming and going at irregular times so all of us had to be constantly on the alert. Jack and I had to stick to certain rules, such as:

1) never leave a room on your own unless you are sure that Frowzy is not in;
2) wait for a signal from one of the family that you can come out if you wish to leave your room, even while the German woman is in;
3) in case you both want to go up or downstairs while she is in, you should tiptoe along the stairs, shoes in hand or walk in the same stride as one man, to avoid attracting attention from old Frowzy.

As regards rule 2) the family had removed a big wardrobe on the landing upstairs, so that it stood close to Frowzy's bedroom door. Whenever we wanted to leave our room while Old Frowzy was hovering about in her room longer than usual, Nancy used to open the right door of the wardrobe, thus covering the entire bedroom door. At the moment we came out of our room, Nancy gestured that everything was O.K., for even if Frau Bohres had heard the wardrobe door being opened and suddenly opened her door (she tended to be very nosey), her view would be blocked by the other one. Once or twice she tried to push her way out but Nancy was leaning heavily against the wardrobe door and said something like, "Sorry, just a moment please, I must get some linen out." She just went on collecting some towels or anything until she knew we had tiptoed downstairs and heard the door of the living room opening and closing behind us.

Every scheme to keep clear of Frowzy seemed to work like clockwork, although there were a few times that something nearly went wrong. One day I came out of the living room and just when I was in the middle of the hall young Frowzy suddenly stepped into the hall as well from the opposite side: she had a key to the front door and had quite unexpectedly come back. She looked very surprised at me but said, "Guten Abend" (good evening) civilly enough. I also mumbled a greeting similar to that and retreated at the same time as calmly as I could before she started a conversation. Everyone was quite upset although later on we had a good laugh about it. Later on, Frowzy spoke to Mr. de Vries and asked him, "Who was that young man whom I met in the hall, who seemed so shy that he turned on his heels after I had only said good evening?" Mr. de Vries had anticipated such a question and told her I was the son of a very dear friend who had died in the early days of war, and that I was staying now for some time only with the family de Vries as I was suffering from nerves since that awful time, being unable to work, and the change of air might do me good. At this quickly cooked-up story Frowzy was nearly moved to tears and she even promised not to breathe a word about this to her superiors.

One of the most bizarre episodes took place each week when young Frowzy had sent from Amsterdam, usually by a sergeant in the German Army, some seafish, which was in those days hardly ever seen in Dutch households. Old Frowzy did not like fish, so she gave it to the family de Vries but they in turn were not keen to accept gifts or favours from a German, so they took great delight in giving all the fish to us. This caused much amusement and satisfaction at the thought of a German soldier bringing this fish all that way to a German woman, while neither of them had an idea that two R.A.F. officers were consuming it heartily.

One morning when Nancy had to take up some drink to the old German woman the latter said moodily, "Did you also hear all those rotten English planes last night again? They have kept me awake nearly the whole night and I just heard over the radio that they bombed my home town Köln (Cologne) quite heavily, those damned English pilots!" When she got downstairs again Nancy excitedly told us this good bit of news. Her Dad remarked dryly, "I do hope you had another expression on your face when Frowzy told you this news."

Strangely enough the German woman often expected sympathy from the people to whom our planes sounded like music, for every time they came droning over at night the Dutch felt encouraged in their hope for better times. During this period we were visited by the Dutch Resistance, namely Dick, who was in communication with

England; and Narda, the 24 year old girl who was the leader in Apeldoorn; later to be betrayed and delivered to the Gestapo who transported her to several concentration camps where she suffered terrible tortures, but miraculously survived. She is still alive today, this very brave girl, and living in Switzerland, the only country where her permanently damaged lungs can breathe enough air.

Dick and Narda told us that it was difficult for them to move us on at that time and that we should have to be patient and await the right moment.

Apart from the members of the Dutch "Underground" we met Mr. de Vries' brother Henk, who was a partner in the same company and Bob's fiancee Daisy, who supplied us with a wide variety of books to read; she used to smuggle them out of her home. We were very appreciative of this as we had lots of time on our hands and being restricted to only certain parts of the house meant our activities were limited. We used to play some games and cards with Bob and Nancy and I helped Nancy with the stringing of beans and collecting and sorting of red currants, strawberries, raspberries and gooseberries, which grew in the garden. We were lucky to have the use of such a large garden, i.e. when the Germans were not at home, for we were able to walk or sit in the sun. If "the coast was not clear" inside the house we were warned by a danger signal, a piece of smoked bacon, hanging on a wall. In such a case we had to hurry inside if we were near the house, or we had to stay away, if the distance would be too far and keep ourselves hidden in the back of the garden. Another advantage was that the German women had a radio in their sitting room, so when they were out we could tune into London and hear the news. The Dutch people were not allowed to listen to or possess a radio (the one of the family de Vries was taken away in the first week of the war (May 1940) as their name was already on the 'black list' of the Germans). This was official but my experience during my time in Holland was that very few homes did not possess one. In many strange places we were able to listen over the next 9 months.

Quite a strange experience to me was having a tooth out in an ordinary chair, painlessly done by an underground dentist. Trust me to get a toothache at this time.

Within a short while of our arrival with the de Vries family, we heard that Ken Ingram, the Flight Engineer, was safe and being looked after by the Resistance in another safe house in Apeldoorn. He was brought over to see us and stayed a few days; his visit was to be the last time we saw him, as will be related in a later episode.

Just when we had been with our helpers for a month we were told that another R.A.F. officer was being brought to the house. He was recovering from injuries obtained when his Halifax was shot down.

This was our first introduction to pilot officer Ken Parsons, whom I would be with for the rest of my stay in Holland, culminating in our escape to the British lines the following March 1945. Ken Parsons stayed with us for a few days and then he went next door to stay with a retired doctor and his wife, who also had a German billeted with them.

On another occasion a member of the American Air Force, Robert Zurcher, who was also hiding somewhere in Apeldoorn, was brought round to see us for a day's visit. Sometimes we used to walk after dark in a lane at the end of the garden, but only a short distance, and any other movement outside the house and garden would have been too dangerous.

Time passed very quickly though, thanks to our hosts, and we were able to introduce some entertaining games unknown to the Dutch whilst of course they did the same with us. I must say that, considering the circumstances, we all had some fun and I believe it brought a little pleasure into the lives of our helpers, breaking the monotony of life during 4 years' occupation by the enemy.

We often wondered whether our folk at home had received any news of our survival. Dick told us that our names had been sent back to England; we were therefore very pleased when Mr. de Vries told us that some English ladies were being repatriated to England in exchange for wounded German prisoners of war. They had been given our names and addresses and asked to contact our relatives when they arrived back home. The result of this was, in my case, that towards the end of November 1944, my parents received a letter from a Mrs. Segar which read as follows (the envelope was addressed to family Blakemore):

> *Dear Friends*
>
> *Firstly I must explain to you that I was an English resident in Holland up to July of this year, since when I have been repatriated to England from an internment camp in France. On my departure from German-occupied Holland, which part unfortunately, is still under*

> German rule, I was asked to convey to you by a very
> good Dutch friend of mine that your son Eric Blakemore
> was, when I left, alive and well and up to that date had
> not fallen into enemy hands.

The letter concluded with best wishes for a speedy reunion.

My parents, on replying to Mrs. Segar who lived in Southampton, invited her and her husband to call and see them if they were ever in Bournemouth. I am glad to say they were able to do this on the 5th December and my parents were able to thank them personally.

It was in August that the Resistance brought to us an injured R.A.F. airman who had been an in-patient at Apeldoorn Hospital with Septicaemia. He had been in hospital under the guise of a Dutchman, but due to the fact that it became common knowledge that he was an allied flier it was imperative he was moved elsewhere. Narda, dressed up as a nurse, and with the help of the resistance workers in the hospital, brought him to Frisolaan 5. He was able to get attention from a specialist and the doctor next door at nr. 7.

George Palamountain, our new evader, was in a very bad way when he arrived and we all thought he would not survive the next few days. In fact I know that preparations were made so that, in the event of his dying, he would be buried in the garden until it was safe to carry out the correct service. This might sound a little callous, but one had to remember this was war time, not fought under the Queensbury rules, and any risk had to be eliminated.

We used to take it in turns to look after George at night and I do remember one night not having any sleeping powder for him, so I pretended to mix a sleeping powder and as there was only a candle to light the room, he could not see the mixture. I was lucky as he slept well all the night through, so a little bit of psychology worked.

George's recovery was very slow, even though he was able to have aid from stolen German drugs. I am glad to say that George survived and was liberated together with the Dutch in Apeldoorn on 17th April 1945. Very soon after that day he returned to Hereford where he and his family are living today.

Our routine was dramatically broken one day when Frau Bohres, the German woman, returned to the house in a great panic, telling Mr. de Vries that the British parachutists had landed near Arnhem and her daughter had told her to pack her belongings and return to Germany at once. The date was 17th September, the start of the attempt to capture the bridge at Arnhem and shorten the war by many months. When we heard the news of the attack we were all thrilled and hoped that it would not be long before freedom came to us all. While we could hear the guns (the distance between Apeldoorn and Arnhem is 20 miles), Nancy optimistically washed the Dutch flag, and even wanted to hang it on the washing line, but Jack prevented this, pointing out that not all the Germans had left yet.

Sadly this was too true, for as we all know, freedom did not reach us yet in those days. The sound of the far-away guns gradually died away and the disaster of the Battle of Arnhem was to be unfolded, with the hopes of millions delayed for several months, not to mention the lives that were to be lost both among the armed forces on both sides and the brave Dutch people.

With the advent of Arnhem, electric supplies were cut off and the only light available was the use of oil lamps and candles; so the life of austerity was to begin which, sadly for the vast majority of the population in occupied Holland was to increase month by month, with the supply of food, especially in the large towns and villages, becoming non-existent as time went on.

To return to the last days of September, we all still hoped that something would be retrieved from Arnhem; and it was at this time that the Resistance in Apeldoorn were planning their next moves, not knowing that they had a traitor in their midst who was only waiting for the Gestapo to arrive and set up their headquarters in our neighbourhood. It would end up in the capture and death of many brave Underground people and also in the brutal killing of two American Air Force members and one R.A.F. member.

The whole dreadful episode started on 30th September with the Gestapo suddenly arresting Narda van Terwisga, the leader of the Apeldoorn Underground movement, in her own home and thereafter sitting back and arresting anybody who called at Narda's home. Unfortunately our host Mr. de Vries was one of those callers and when he had not returned after several hours, Nancy went out at curfew time, then at 10 p.m. to try and find him. (Resistance workers often did not even tell their own family when or where they had a meeting for safety's sake.) Eventually she also called at Narda's home and was immediately arrested and questioned like all the other people.

Near midnight they were brought over to the large house in the neighbourhood, taken over by the Gestapo. The place was crowded with the latter and extremely well guarded by them, even along the road and round the park, where the house was situated.

After more questioning, one Gestapo man shouted that there were "too many of these damned people in this place" so a few, who seemed fairly innocent, were selected to leave the building, amongst them Mr. de Vries and his daughter. Unfortunately at the last moment someone discovered a false document (made by the Resistance) in Mr. de Vries's wallet so he was detained.

Nancy ran home as fast as she could as soon as she was out of sight of the Gestapo, hoping they had not sent some men to Frisolaan 5 yet in order to arrest everybody over there as well. We were all shattered by her news, although with the non-return of both Nancy and her father it was obvious that something terrible had happened. So Jack and I with Ken Parsons had moved further down the road and hidden in a greenhouse, belonging to a retired clergyman. That night we slept at nr. 7 with Ken and awaited the outcome of the next day, Sunday October 1st.

In the morning George was carried from Frisolaan 5 to nr. 7 and installed in the attic bedroom that Ken had been using; this at least left the house clear of any suspects. Then we were told that as soon as it could be arranged we would be escorted out of Apeldoorn on bicycles, along the road by the Apeldoornsch Canal, Northwards in the direction of Epe. (This was the road that Jack and I had used in June, which seemed a backward step, but absolutely necessary.) No further information was given at that time but we were to learn later that we would be picked up by a fire engine and taken to Epe.

Just after twelve o'clock Mr. de Vries came home suddenly, shocked and exhausted by all the hours' questioning. He was set free only temporarily, in order to find the person responsible for making those false documents, having to report to the Gestapo again within 2 days, "else they would arrest and punish the whole family". Around one o'clock we set off with our escort, comprising Bob, Daisy and another resistance member, Mr. Jansen, assistant manager to Mr. de Vries at Venz, the chocolate factory.

It seemed to me a very sad moment to be leaving the family without being able to do anything and not knowing what the outcome would be; we seemed so helpless, yet the sooner we went away, the better it would be for our helpers, who would have to "go under water" as the Resistance expression was for leaving one's home and hiding somewhere, without leaving a trace. (Later on several attempts were made by the Gestapo to arrest the family at Frisolaan 5, but fortunately they had fled by then.)

Thus ended our stay in Apeldoorn, certainly not the way we had hoped, especially when we learnt later on that the Gestapo had caught our crew member Kenneth Ingram and two American fliers; and instead of making them prisoners of war they had ruthlessly killed them, leaving them in the road, with the label of "Terrorist", just like they did with several Dutch Resistance people.

This shows that the Germans were not only carrying out their cruel "task" in the concentration camps but were equally capable of doing this in the middle of a Dutch town. I only hope that the men responsible for this were later caught and received whatever punishment they deserved.

It was raining when we left Apeldoorn. In about ten minutes we were out of town and found ourselves, according to plan, back on the road along the Apeldoorns Canal, by which we had come to Apeldoorn, just over 3 months ago. We saw no Germans and after nearly 6 kilometres we dismounted and hid our bicycles in the rushes at the roadside. Then we just stood there, huddled together in the rain, awaiting the fire brigade.

Sure enough, after half an hour, the bell was heard in the distance so we said goodbye to our escort. While the fire engine drew up, firemen's helmets and clothing were thrown to us which we were to put on obviously. At this moment I noticed some people in the barges which were moored on the Canal, watching us with amazement and curiosity. We hastily struggled into the leather jackets and donned fire fighting helmets (which seemed too small for us), and meanwhile the fire engine made a swift turn round and drove back to us. As soon as we had climbed aboard it raced off in the direction of Epe, its bell clanging loudly to pretend we were really going to fight a fire somewhere.

I was on the rearside and all I can remember is hanging on like grim death as the telegraph poles flashed so close by. (The fire engines in those days were open where the firemen stood on a platform on each side hanging on to a rail.) I can honestly say that I was as scared as I ever had been, even on operations. We eventually arrived in Epe and drove straight into the fire station where we were quickly put in a car driven by the same fireman who had driven the fire engine; in fact we learnt later that it was owned by him.

After a short ride out of Epe we turned off into a large wood, split into sections which were separated by a fire track, at last stopping at one section deep inside the wood.

We left the car and walked a short distance, a spot where the planting of the trees was very dense, making it impossible for anyone to see through them. There we disappeared into the darkness until we came across a wooden hut buried in the ground with just the roof showing. The roof itself was covered with turf, branches and other parts of trees, making it invisible from the air. Inside the hut were a table and sleeping bunks for six people. After having introduced us to the other three occupants, who were young Dutchmen living underground in order to escape transportation to forced labour camps, our escort left us. We were then taken further into the woods where another hut housed a Jewish family, comprising father, mother and two young daughters.

The camp was known in those days as "Pas Op" (meaning "be careful"); today it is called "the Hidden Village" due to the fact that there were three other encampments in three other sections of the woods, sheltering some 60 odd people.

The food was brought by bicycle from a nearby village, which must have been a tremendous task and indeed was a brave effort: not only to obtain the food but also to arrange the transport unnoticed by other people.

The "Pas Op Camp" or "Hidden Village" was the brainchild of a retired railwayman, known to us as Opa Bakker and his housekeeper "Tante Cong". Tragically Mr. Bakker was eventually caught by the Germans and killed, but Tante Cong escaped and is still alive today, I am happy to say.

Our stay at "Pas Op" was to last nearly four weeks, which for me was the worst part of our entire stay in Holland, owing to the lack of being able to exercise and the impossibility to do anything other than talk. Perhaps it was also due to the feeling of being shut in amongst the trees, for the only unobstructed view was high up towards the sky.

We did have one scare during the day when we thought that there were Germans approaching. We all moved quickly to other parts of the wood, returning after a short while, however, when it turned out to be a false alarm.

Regretfully a few weeks later the camp was indeed discovered by the Germans, although most of the occupants escaped, including the Jewish family. However, much to our grief, as previously mentioned, Opa Bakker was captured and shot by the Germans. After our hurried departure from "Pas Op" we went to various short-stay addresses, safe houses like one on the edge of the former Zuiderzee (now the Isselneer).

Jack and I also stayed with one lady who, unfortunately during our sojourn, was suddenly visited by a German officer. He strode through the whole house, taking not the slightest interest in us and merely acknowledging us with a polite "Good morning".

He spoke to the owner of the house for some time and then departed. He had been looking for accommodation only and demonstrated to us a characteristic of the Germans: their single-mindedness. Whenever they were looking for bicycles, or accommodation or young people for work gangs, they concentrated on the task on hand only and showed no interest whatsoever in anything else. If the German had been looking for young men or escapers then he would most certainly have shown interest in us.

Naturally after this episode we had to move on as understandably our hostess had become very nervous. We met up again with Ken Parsons and a Captain Noble who was a doctor in the Airborne Division, having escaped from Arnhem. One of the safe houses we stayed in for a few hours was a very large mansion, where the sons had constructed a firing range underground, so that the Resistance could practice.

During the month of October, a successful crossing was made over the Rhine, east of Arnhem, by the remnants of the Airborne Army and any other Allied personnel. This was called "Operation Pegasus", taking place on the night of 22nd October. Over 150 men were taken across the river.

Many were still left behind and were hidden by the Dutch people who had also suffered heavily in the battles for the town and bridges. It was decided to try the same operation again on 22nd November, a little premature considering the Germans would still be on the lookout for any Allied troops, which they had not caught yet. It was arranged that this crossing would include any Allied evaders, so we were gathered together near Elburg, dressed like Dutch workers being taken for forced labour to strengthen the defences near Arnhem.

The journey was made mostly in the dark, in a stolen German lorry, driven by a Dutchman. We passed through a number of check points and arrived on a spot several miles away from the proposed crossing, only to find to our dismay that the party had already left. We dispersed into the surrounding woods, about 15 to 20 of us, mostly Airborne personnel. While waiting there, feeling very depressed and disappointed, we suddenly heard machine gun fire from the direction of the river, which sounded quite ominous. In the next days we learnt the sorrowful news that the party were ambushed and had to scatter: several men were killed, many of them were captured and only a few managed to escape and find help from the Resistance.

With this sad news we realised how lucky we were to have been late and miss this party. Our feeling of disappointment changed into one of thankfulness for having escaped this tragedy. As previously mentioned the organisers were still not convinced that the Germans were a hard, dedicated and certainly not stupid sort, who would become even tougher opponents as we came nearer to their fatherland.

We had to spend the next few days sheltering in the woods. Unfortunately it was raining which, together with the lack of food, added to our misery. At last the Resistance found all of us again and revived us with some hot food and schnapps. They did a wonderful job in keeping us supplied until they had arranged to take us by horse and wagon with a tarpaulin over us to an isolated barn where we had to stay for the next few days before a safe house was found for each of us.

Ken Parsons and myself were extremely lucky to be taken to the house of the Christen family in Barneveld where we were able to have a bath and a shave for the first time in many days.

The Christen family were eight in number: Father Piet, Mother Jet and 6 children with ages ranging from 15 to a baby of a few months, named Hans. The others were Pim, Djoeky, Filkie, Conny and Niki, so there were 4 girls, one boy plus a baby-boy. When we arrived the children were having a party (I think it was Saint Nicholas Day, 6th December), so we were rushed upstairs until it was over (shades of Apeldoorn), and then we came down and met the family.

Piet Christen was actually a teacher of German but nobody wished to learn it now, so he taught English instead. He was glad of the opportunity to practise with us and gave us a few lessons in Dutch.

I do remember vividly that during our stay with this family we walked one Sunday afternoon with them all around the streets; it seemed that everyone was out walking on that fine afternoon.

There was not a single German in sight and as it was the first time we had had a walk since landing in Holland it made us almost forget the war, just for a little while anyway.

Unfortunately we heard that the Christen's maid had been seen fraternising with German soldiers which caused us to leave the day before Christmas: she might talk about us. I shall always admire the courage of Mr. and Mrs. Christen giving us a shelter at such a risk to themselves. They certainly had a great faith in their children keeping quiet about us and I do not know how they managed. It is extremely hard to keep exciting news even for grown-ups, let alone for young school children.

We were taken out of Barneveld to a farm for a day or two and I do remember Christmas Day: the only sign of it was made by Ken, playing a carol on an old piano with one finger. Our hosts did not seem to take much notice, but then we did not know what worrying thoughts about this last grim winter of the occupation were crossing their minds. (It was to be the notorious hunger winter for Holland.)

Our next hiding place was with a Mr. and Mrs. Overeem in Voorthuisen, where I learnt to play bridge (well, a little anyhow). I also made butter and I read the two books "She" and "The return of She".

CHAPTER 7

1945

We celebrated the New Year with our hosts, producing their last luxuries, i.e. some tinned sausages and a bottle of cognac. They knew that this would be their last New Year's Eve under the Germans and so they shared this special food and drink with us.

We were astonished to hear many planes on New Year's Day, which turned out to be the last effort by the Luftwaffe. They just put up every plane they had and I learnt from later reports that they caught the Allies on the hop, causing a fair amount of damage in some places. However, the German losses were high, probably due to a lot of old aircraft having been used. (Shades of our first 1000 bomber raid!)

One cold night a party of German soldiers came knocking on the door. Ken and I immediately jumped out of bed and went hurriedly through the window into the snow. We ran towards a wood close by, where we remained hidden for some time. We were only wearing short pants so you can imagine that we were nearly frozen. Unfortunately the Germans only wanted an address of a former guest at the house and did not enter the premises at all. As soon as they had left we quickly returned to our beds and soon forgot the cold; also it was quite a relief to know that our hosts would be safe after all.

This incident naturally upset our host's wife, so we had to move on again to another safe place the following day.

All our moves were made mostly at night by bicycle. (The Dutch cars were either taken away, or rather stolen, by the gradually retreating Germans or they were hidden somewhere from the latter.)

As I was a poor cyclist you can understand how I suffered! The worst trip was one night when we were moving from one safe house to another along a road which, like everywhere in Holland, had a cycle track. This special track was separated from the road by short tree stumps.

The usual practice was for one Dutch guide to be in front and one behind. Suddenly the guide at the back told us to hurry as she thought she had heard Germans behind us, so everybody pedalled faster. Unfortunately I hit one of the tree stumps and went flying, landing heavily on my right shoulder. I got up and quickly remounted my bicycle, chasing after the others. The pain in my shoulder was excruciating, but the thought of the Germans behind us put the pain in the background, which only proves how fear can overcome any adversity. After a while, however, it appeared that there was no one following us at all, so it had been a false alarm. My shoulder was painful for several weeks, which necessitated shaking hands with my left hand, like in the days of being a Boy Scout.

After leaving Voorthuizen we found ourselves in various safe houses, two of which remain in my memory. The first one was a small farm where we had to sleep above the cows which did not worry us at all. However, during the night we heard other creatures moving around which turned out to be rats; they even crept over us which we thought quite gruesome.

In the daytime we tried our hand at milking and threshing wheat; I must say that the latter was more successful than the former; even though it was January, the flies were there in force and used to get in any drink we had. The only way to satisfy one's thirst was to blow them to one side and then take a quick gulp!

The second safe house was another small farm where I was staying at this time with a glider pilot, Captain Angus Lowe, while Ken had gone to another address nearby. In this place we helped to turn sugar beet into treacle, which was quite an interesting process. The sugar beet by now was nearly the only food available on the ration cards. It was awful to see young girls from the large towns, having to beg for food at the farms. They offered anything valuable they might possess, for money was not acceptable any more. Everyone knew that all the "Dutch" or rather German money would be exchanged soon after Liberation. (The Germans had claimed all the Dutch silver money soon after they occupied Holland, substituting it by cheap looking nickel coins.)

Another reason for not accepting money at that time was the fact that (like in other countries) there was a Black Market where some people had made their fortunes; once the exchange of money would be made in the near future anybody with large amounts would have to explain where they got that from during the occupation.

Apart from all this there was hardly anything left to buy, as the Germans had taken most of the food, clothing etc., so the Dutch tried to trade for instance soap for sugar, a bicycle for a few potatoes etc.

We were very fortunate that the people who looked after us saw that we always had sufficient to eat and were always willing to share whatever they had with us.

Later on we were told that the Underground movement used to steal back Dutch food from German transport, simply by holding up the Germans by shooting at them. At that time the 'Wehrmacht' was not as heavily armed as they used to be and the Underground used to round up war-weary Germans who were only to willing to exchange their uniforms and everything with it for civilian clothes, fairly human treatment and some rest.

The German uniforms and eventual rifles etc. came in extremely handy for the Underground movement. If there were unwilling Germans who would not cooperate and proved to become a danger, they were shot.

It was during this period that we were introduced to an Army officer who was being hidden in a large house; only many years later a colleague at work told me that he had seen my name mentioned in a book, called "The Grey Goose", an account of General Sir John Hackett's escape after the battle at Arnhem. At the time Sir John was a Brigadier and his identity was carefully kept secret in order to avoid attracting any attention since he was a wanted man by the Germans.

The extract from the book related to a beadle, locking the door of an empty church after the Sunday service and then climbing some stone stairs behind the pulpit. Subsequently he opened a secret panel above the organ keyboard and switched on the radio for the 9 p.m. B.B.C. news from London! Sitting on the floor in the loft, also eagerly waiting for the evening broadcast were: Flying officers Kenneth Parsons, Eric Blakemore and James Branford of the R.A.F.

After the news the beadle left the church and went to his house where the tired General Hackett had arrived. Soon the other men in the loft would surreptitiously come down and join the Brigadier to exchange news and gossip and have a drink of egg flip. One day, after an exhausting journey between some safe houses, I had grown so tired that I only wanted to lie down and sleep, even when at last news came that three out of the five of us could go ahead to the river for a crossing. I quickly volunteered to stay as I badly needed sleep then and there. I believe that if the Germans had been coming I would not even have had the energy to move away from them. I can well imagine how Scott and his companions felt on their journey back from the South Pole.

However the three returned after a few hours but were unable to cross a bridge which proved to be guarded by the Germans.

A new plan was prepared and the next day we moved further south on our way to Sliedrecht, to a riverside house from where we would try and leave occupied Holland down the river to the Allies.

We reached the riverside house early in the morning and even though we were looking rather unclean, due to lack of washing facilities, the host insisted on us sleeping in what seemed to us absolute luxury: beds with clean sheets.

That night we crept from the house to a rowing boat with muffled oars and met our guides who were going to take us to the Hollandsch Diep and back up the Maas to Lage Zwaluwe, to freedom.

We donned our safety jackets and all of us were ready for our last journey, away from the Germans. I clearly remember the quite peculiar smell of British cigarettes which had been smoked in the room, while we were waiting for our guides. My cigarettes for the past months had been, when available, tobacco leaves, chopped and rolled in ordinary paper. These were extremely strong compared with British cigarettes, the latter smelling very sickly and weak. In fact I wondered if I would ever like them again but after a few days back in England, I had no problem whatsoever. Strangely enough I have never smelt that certain cigarette scent again since that very last night in Holland.

We were told before starting our journey that we would have to pass a German post and later join other boats. I was allocated to a guide who had a two man canoe with a small engine. I had hardly ever been in a canoe, so I had obtained very little practice in paddling. (My guide told me after we had arrived in Allied lines that he had soon realised that I was not a good canoeist.)

In this way we set off paddling on March 9/10 in the pitch-black night, for indeed very little could be seen. We did not hear a sound from the German post, nor did we see any other boats or canoes after all.

I think the journey took about 2 or 3 hours; I remember being quite surprised about how quickly the time went and much sooner than expected we had arrived on the riverbank, occupied by the Allies. We were free at last after nearly 9 months. It was extremely difficult to realise that we had left all the misery behind us and it seemed like a wonderful dream, too good to be true.

We climbed ashore and awaited the others before going to a building, where we gathered with our guides. After much handshaking we were drinking a good number of toasts with glasses of cognac which combined with an empty stomach and great excitement made us soon feel rather merry.

Our next move was by a jeep to Tilburg and all I can remember is shouting "Good morning" in Dutch to all the people we passed and singing the usual songs.

We were taken to a house in Tilburg where we would be closely interrogated by M 19. First of all, however, we had a hot bath and a hearty breakfast. After all these gratifying matters like cognac, bath and breakfast, I can only dimly remember going to the toilet and locking the door. Thereupon I fell soundly asleep on the seat, fully dressed, only to wake up to loud shouts (both at the window and the door) of, "Eric, are you all right?" They all thought I was ill and had passed out.

We spent the next two days being interrogated, although Ken and I did manage to have a walk round the town, which seemed very strange after having been always on the inside, looking out. I should mention that the only clothes we had at that time were a plain khaki uniform and a civilian hat, not any sign of rank, etc.; therefore we certainly must have looked a very unusual collection of men!

On the 12th March we were told that we would be flown back to England on that same day. Sure enough, at 11 a.m. we set off for the airfield, which possessed merely a few buildings, since it had been the centre of a fierce battle some months ago.

We went to a wooden building, where we had to wait along with many other active service personnel, mostly of high rank and staff officers. When we entered they all looked quite astonished at seeing four individuals dressed in khaki and wearing no hats (Capt. Angus Lowe had a trilby). To say the least, we positively did not look on the same level as the other passengers. After a short wait, an R.A.F. officer entered the room saying that there were 4 vacancies on the next flight: Priority One only. This meant the four of us and he duly called our rank and name: "Captain Lowe, Flight Lieutenant Branford, Flying Officer Blakemore and Pilot Officer Parsons."

I can still see the expression on the faces of those high ranking officers, their mouths dropped open with utter amazement. "Four improperly dressed men Priority No. 1! How on earth could this happen?" they undoubtedly must have thought and, "What is the war coming to?!"

We walked out to the Dakota on that bright sunny morning with a feeling of elation at the thought of going home now at last. The flight was uneventful and it was a wonderful sight to see the white cliffs of Dover, standing out proudly in the sunlight. We crossed the coast west of Dover and landed at the famous fighter station Biggin Hill in Kent.

I cannot describe the feeling I had when our aircraft touched down and we knew that we were home. In our enthusiasm on setting foot on British soil once again, we knelt down and kissed the earth, a procedure which would be used in the future by more eminent persons than we.

We were accompanied to an office where we had to wait for transport to Croydon and from there we would catch a coach for Victoria Station. At Croydon the Customs and Excise officer made quite sure that we had nothing to "declare"! (A bit of a joke this seemed, for our possessions were merely what we stood up in.)

The journey to Victoria Station proved to be an odd experience to us for a while. To be able to mingle with a large crowd and walk freely was such a relief that we must have looked strange creatures with an appearance of awe and wonderment.

Finally we arrived at Victoria Station, where we suddenly decided, even though we had no proper uniforms and Captain Lowe was still wearing his trilby hat, to walk the entire length of the station to the Railway Transport Office to see if we would be apprehended by the Military Police. The latter, as everyone will remember, were usually present at London Terminals in large numbers, but to our disappointment and surprise we did not see any of them!

We said farewell to Angus and then reported to the R.A.F. section who had transport waiting to take us to the M 19 Interrogating Officer No. 107 P.R.C. in Baker Street. We were booked in and had our first pint of English beer for nine months.

After a good night's sleep we spent the day being interviewed regarding several matters, the main interview being a full medical inspection to see if we were fit enough to go home on leave. I should have mentioned that on arrival we were allowed to send telegrams home to say we were safe and hoping to see our families soon. It must have been a great relief to our families to know we were safe, as they had not received any news since November 1944, when all they learnt then was that we were alive and free.

At last, on the 14th March, we were permitted to go on leave, so I said good-bye to Ken Parsons and left Baker Street to visit my sister and her family in North London. In fact, quite unknowingly, I gave my brother-in-law a rather shocking surprise when I phoned to let the family know I was back in England. They only knew that I had been missing since June 1944 and, having learnt no more, they presumed that I was dead! (The R.A.F. had advised my parents to treat all news as confidential until I was safe.)

I was given seven weeks' leave and then was told to report to 106 P.R.C. R.A.F. Cosford. P.R.C., short for Personnel Rehabilitation Centre, which was actually destined for the prisoners of war who had been away for many years. We were the first to go through the routine.

I left London on the 15th March to return to my home in Bournemouth once again. It seemed a whole lifetime, not merely nine months, since I had last made the journey. It was a peculiar feeling to return and be in the familiar surroundings that had been often in one's thoughts, yet had seemed so far away. I can well imagine how the prisoners of war felt when returning from the camps in Japan or Germany after years of deprivation. How wonderful to be home again, to be sleeping in one's own bed, being with your own folk again and being able to walk freely in the streets, meeting people who thought you were one of the missing, never to return service personnel.

I spent my time very quietly, gradually releasing the tension which had been building up over the last months.

I should like to mention that during my period of being missing, my parents had a lot of kind support, especially from Mr. T. C. Dugdale who sent them a framed sketch he had done when painting the crew at Honington in 1941, and who, on seeing the report in the papers that I was back in England, quickly sent a telegram of congratulations on my return. Also Mrs. Pickard (Group Captain Pickard's mother) and Lady Hardwicke (Helena Pickard, his sister), who had met my parents in Bournemouth during the previous nine months and had been very kind and sympathetic despite their great loss. They also sent a telegram expressing their joy.

There were many other people who were also generous in their sympathy and understanding, which at that period was probably at its highest due to the forward push in France, Belgium and Holland.

I was informed during the first leave that a further 21 days had been granted and subsequently I had to report to Cosford on the 18th May.

Now to many people so much leave may seem a most generous gesture by the R.A.F. (7 weeks in all), yet the first 28 days was quite enough for me, really, for I was anxious to have a job to do and occupy my mind to the full.

I had spent all the previous months with only two objects in view, i.e. survival and return to England. What I needed now was responsibility and work for the brain in order to forget the past tension and worry. I do not think this was realised by the powers that be, that the majority of returning prisoners and evaders needed the same. Obviously the thought was that the more leave given was for the best.

I reported to Cosford and was posted the next day to 109 P.C. at Wittering near Stanford. With about nine other aircrew we spent a very leisurely 3 weeks having lectures, taking part in sport and enjoying ourselves in a relaxing atmosphere. We were all being monitored by medical personnel to ensure that our rehabilitation was proceeding on the right lines; as I stated before this treatment was more appropriate for long-serving prisoners of war.

During the three weeks, we were asked to list in order of priority the next trades or jobs we would prefer to do in the R.A.F. or whether we would like to be demobilised; the war in Europe was now at an end, thus operational flying was finished for us. Furthermore we received a list of trades available. I had previously requested to join Transport Command and assist the R.A.F. in their task in Europe, chiefly to help the Dutch people.

This request was never considered, even though I made three visits to the Air Ministry and saw faceless people, who never seemed interested in my request. My idea was to do something useful to help the nation who had looked after me so well.

We were told that we would most probably get the first request we had listed, but most certainly the second; yet all I can say is that I got the fifth and last request granted: a Flying Control Course, which was not exactly what I really wanted. I had applied for a permanent commission and wished to return to Accountancy, which had been No. 1 in my list of three. I did enquire as to the reason why I got the last request, but received no satisfactory explanation, except for their need for aircrew in Flying Control.

My posting arrived while I was on a further 7 day's leave. I had to report to Bramcote, near Nuneaton, to await a course at the Flying Control school at Watchfield near Swindon, which came through a few days later on 18th June.

I have to be honest and admit that I was not wholehearted in taking this course on. I had no keen interest in what would turn out to be a shift occupation; on the contrary, I had applied for an accounting course to avoid that. Moreover accountancy was my vocation since leaving college.

Nevertheless, the other members of the course were good company, which is more than I can say of the instructors! The latter seemed to live in a world of their own, treating the pupils as a breed beneath their level. This was rather amusing, since most of the course members were experienced aircrew, who had survived the horrific rate of casualties in Bomber Command.

The food and accommodation were appalling. I was told that it was a private company, leased to the Air Ministry for the duration of the war, and that the Managing Director was the Commanding Officer of the school; one could certainly draw a conclusion from this, right or wrong.

The course proved to be interesting and straight forward, but I did not care for the flying. I realised then that flying was no longer a pleasure nor exciting, and since that course, I have never again left the ground. I decided that fate had been kind to me and for this reason should not be provoked.

The exams and tests on the course were not too difficult and I passed all of them, except the last one, which was an oral test. There was a very simple reason for this: I was called into the room to be questioned by an extremely arrogant and self opinionated squadron leader, no doubt well versed in flying control procedures, but having absolutely no idea regarding behaviour towards ex-aircrew.

I had, on returning to England, realised that I had become a very impatient person, rather short-tempered and too outspoken. I used to say whatever I thought about an irritating situation or anything like that, probably with a sharp intonation as well.

After I had entered the room and sat down in the chair provided, I had to listen to the instructor's conversation with a friend about his pending demobilisation and return to traffic control in civilian life. This went on for over 20 minutes, which infuriated me to such an extent that I asked him how much longer I would be kept waiting, as I could find better things to do. Without an apology he said that he would start the questions right now. I answered most of them, but knew that he would fail me anyhow on the question of attitude, which he did.

I was not unduly disappointed, for I knew I was not a failed pupil in reality; but as I was not keen on this occupation it might enable me to obtain work which I really wanted.

I returned to Bramcote and carried out administration duties while awaiting a further posting to Catterick for further interviews regarding the eventual course I would next proceed to.

I constantly reminded the interviewers of my first choice, and at last after an interview at the Air Ministry with a senior officer of the Accounting section, I was promised a place on a course. In the meantime, however, I would be posted near home at Holmsley south near Christchurch in the Accounts, to await a vacancy at the school of Administration and Accounts.

At long last, on the 8th October, I arrived at Holmsley South and reported to the Accounts, where I was going to receive a thorough grounding in the strange accounting methods and systems of the R.A.F.

On my second day I was asked by the senior accounting officer whether I had ever taken a pay parade. On telling him I had not, he quickly replied that I would take one that day, by paying out the airwomen at their parade. This was something I had not expected and I can honestly say I had never been so nervous as I was then, despite previous exploits. Fortunately everything went off well, although being the only male amongst 400 females is an unusual experience. I was informed at the Air Ministry that my posting near home would enable me to live out from the station if I wanted, but when I made enquiries at Holmsley I learnt that the Commanding Officer of the station did not allow single officers to live out.

It was rather unfortunate that we had a C.O. who was desperate to get back to peace time rules and regulations, failing to understand that those days were over and a new breed would soon be occupying the senior posts.

I was still awaiting my course when Christmas and the New Year arrived, which were spent at home for the first time in peace. Even though food and the usual Christmas luxuries were not available, we all had a good time, a very sharp contrast to the same days in 1944.

CHAPTER 8

1946

Everything continued very much the same for the first few weeks of 1946, until, at last, I was told to report to the school of Administration and Accounts at Hereford on the 8th February. I arrived full of hope and was eagerly looking forward to finally getting down to a course which would result in a proper position, instead of an odd job. Imagine my astonishment, on arriving at Hereford, to find the course was just for Administration, not Accounts!

An error in my posting had been made and I would have to return to Holmsley and await an Accounts course.

I could not believe it, but my wish for a permanent career in the R.A.F. was rapidly being eroded.

Two further incidents convinced me eventually that regular service was not my scene. The first incident occurred when I wanted to join 246 squadron of Transport Command, which was stationed at Holmsley. They were on regular flights to India, bringing back the troops from the Far and Middle East. I naturally had my friends in the Squadron and they asked me to do a trip with them; they would fix me up with tropical kit etc. I was extremely keen to test my senses and nerves for a long flight and see if I was still O.K. I endeavoured to get H.Q.'s permission but my request was turned down flat by the C.O.

The second incident happened when for the first and only time I was Orderly Officer. One of the duties was to inspect the defaulters in the guard room at 22.30. The guard room was one mile up the road from the Officers Mess. As the rain was pouring down at the time when I should report, I rang the Transport Section for transport up to the Guard Room. I was informed that this was not permitted, so I could not have any transport.

I enquired by whom the emergency transport requests were signed, at which a prompt answer came: "By the Orderly Officer, sir." Thereupon I told them to fill in the relevant form, then I would sign it and so I would not get wet.

The transport duly arrived, though very reluctantly, I may add. The next day I was told by the Station Adjutant that the Commanding

Officer wished to see me and the latter gave me a lecture on "behaving like an officer, by keeping to the rules and regulations", in other words: I should have walked in the rain.

To me this definitely was the last straw, for if this was to be life in the R.A.F. in peace time, I wanted none of it. Thus, on the way out I collected a form for demobilisation, which I was entitled to, filled it in at once, had it signed and awaited my release.

This duly arrived after a few weeks and I reported to Uxbridge where 7 years prior I had done the same thing, although not only in different circumstances but now also as a very much changed person.

Perhaps my action in leaving seemed an act of cutting off my nose to spite my face but I do know that I was feeling mixed up, and only then did I become aware of the after effect of war, the strain of the previous years.

If only I had been given a proper responsible job; it was already over one year since returning to England! I do appreciate that this period must have been a big effort on the postings branch, what with so many persons being demobilised, yet it is natural to think that you are the only one.

So I left the R.A.F. at Uxbridge with my demob suit and papers, thus finishing the "seven years interlude". A new life was lying before me and I would endeavour to make the best of it. I can say now that I have not regretted my decision, so maybe the events were in my favour and destiny does play a big part in one's life. At least I was still alive and fairly fit, a privilege which had been denied to many of my colleagues.

CHAPTER 9

Conclusion

Undoubtedly like thousands of other servicemen, I have wondered over the last 40 years what effect the war actually had on our lives. What would have happened if we had not been called on to serve our country and help to destroy the evil, which had for a second time reared its ugly head in Germany? Of course no one knows, therefore this question will remain unanswered.

In my case the experience of those 7 years proved to be in some respects beneficial, whereas in another respect, it meant a downright set-back because of the loss of seven years, which might have been the most important for building a career and a future life.

I realised when leaving the Royal Air Force that I would not be returning to my former employer, as I did not want to live or work in London. Besides, I could not picture myself cooped up in a London office every day, with my present mood, not to mention my tense and rather introvert feelings.

What were the benefits of those seven years? In the first place, like all combined exercises or experiences it was the comradeship which can be found in no other sphere; at least in my experience of being amongst such a cross section of the community, finding such unselfish, honest and friendly attitudes was quite incredible.

After having been at school and a couple of years in the City as a trainee, the whole aspect of life was expanded to the very distant extremes. Once you are dependent on, and responsible for each other in the matter of life and death, only then you will be able to see your fellow human beings come out in their true colours.

My life has been saved several times by many people and I do hope that, in a small way, I may have done the same thing. The outcome of all this was, like in many other cases, not a gradual ageing but a rapid change from a happy-go-lucky personality to a serious one, perhaps not a bad thing in some respect, or even rather an asset.

The one benefit I have always felt was that I had learnt to make decisions myself and not to rely constantly on someone else to agree. I have noticed in my later years in business how few people in responsible positions dare to commit themselves to a decision, which probably explains our lamentable lack of capable top management. Now we have come to the final analysis of the "seven years interlude":

Was there a general feeling of a job well done? What satisfaction could be derived from the results? Could we be proud of the contribution made by Bomber Command?

I think that the job carried out by the Command was of the highest order, despite the murmurings and grumblings from the critics. Maybe the results obtained were not as good as one would have wished, but these were surely due to the higher Command and not to the aircraft and their gallant crews.

Max Hastings, in his book "Bomber Command", states that: "Bomber Command was very well served by its aircrew and, with a few exceptions, very badly served by its senior officers." For the handful of senior officers directly concerned with the planning of operations, High Wycombe was a fascinating posting; for those of less exalted rank it was a staid, formal claustrophobic place. Young wing commanders posted to High Wycombe from ops yearned to escape, their opinions and advice were seldom heeded: not unlike a famous German general in the first World War, who referred to the British Army as "Lions, led by donkeys".

There has always been a widespread rumour that Bomber Commands Commander-in-Chief Arthur Harris was immensely popular with the bomber crews. I find that difficult to believe as I never heard or noticed anything about this reputed popularity on the squadrons. The Group Commanders certainly were popular, but how could a man who never bothered to visit his squadrons possibly be popular? He was generally known as "Butch Harris".

I suppose that the only aircrew who looked upon him as such a great man were those who joined the Command near the end of the war, and used to join the reunions afterwards, indulging themselves in more alcoholic drinks than was necessary. I wonder what the 65,000 casualties (this represented almost 50%) would have said about this? I simply cannot understand how a man in command could retire to bed without a qualm! It is one of the ironies of the bomber offences that while the aircrew fought through the darkness over Germany with the blinding searchlights and the enemy fighters around them plus the nightly torment and blast of the Ach Ach guns, the Commander-in-Chief of Bomber Command lay dreamless in his bed amongst the Buckinghamshire woods.

How much thought was given to the risk chances of the crews when they were sent on their operations? I can merely quote from the Bomber Command's report of night operation on 21/22 June 1944, the night in which I was shot down: out of 265 aircraft, 45 were lost, which is 17%!

The weather forecast was such that the targets were expected to remain clear all night; as it was, all the targets were covered in thick low clouds, while the German fighters found our aircraft very easy targets against the bright midsummer sky! In other words, the odds were stacked against us, as I am positive they were on many other occasions.

All this gives the impression of a Somme-like attitude which was shown towards the losses as if targets must be attacked at all costs and under any conditions. Despite the critics at the end of the war and since, at least the crews knew that they were keeping up the morale, not only of the people being bombed by the Germans, but also in the Occupied countries. The latter felt that Germany was receiving something which served her right, after having bombed Warsaw, Rotterdam and other European towns ruthlessly. Moreover, the British air raids in Germany gave them hope and a firm belief that one day freedom would really be gained in this way.

This was brought home to me during my recent visit to Holland, when I was told that Dutch people used to listen eagerly to hear whether the R.A.F. would come flying over again to Germany at night. They tried to "count" the numbers of aircraft, keeping their fingers crossed for them and in their minds they were with them. When the brave tommies came at last droning back, everyone prayed for their safe homecoming.

I know people will say that I have been too critical of those at the top and ask why I should be justified in this criticism, especially after forty years. All I can say is that I am surely entitled to do so as one of the many whose lives were either mentally or physically affected, or even (as in numerous cases) finished, by the decisions at the top.

It would seem that the real commanders, that is those on the squadrons, were not involved in the decision making, either because they did not survive or were looked upon as too young and inexperienced.

It must have been difficult for the service chiefs to realise that wars are no longer won on the playing fields of Eton but on the Canadian prairies, or the Australian and New Zealand plains; plus in the case of the lower middle class of the United Kingdom, on the Grammar and Secondary school playing fields. I even read somewhere that when the Royal Air Force wanted to intensify its bombing, the other services were reluctant to cooperate, in case the war might be finished without them obtaining any glory.

Thank God this only happened at the top; the admiration and delight when any success was achieved by any of the services was shared by all, but the men in their ivory towers.

It seems rather ironic to me that there is nowadays so much talk about reconciliation and about the fact that we only fought the Nazis and not the Germans. This is of course ridiculous as, apart from the few, all the Germans were in favour of Hitler, especially since he had brought so much "lory" to the Fatherland. Only when they realised they could not win the war did their attitudes change.

I exclude all the evil of the concentration camps from this, for I am positive that the large majority would have been horrified if they had known.

We only have to trace history back to the 1914/1918 World War to find Kaiser Wilhelm and his minions with the same evil (and typically German!) ambitions. The subsequent failure and complete deterioration of the German Reich formed an incentive for Hitler and his party, with more success, at least in the beginning. At any rate, we shall be safe from any further aggression of the Germans, now that the Federation of Europe is possible. Apart from that they seem to have done better than we on the industrial front at all levels.

I have revisited Holland after 40 years and had several joyful reunions with my helpers and resistance workers.

One visit was to the Fire Brigade at Epe, where I had the pleasure of meeting the driver of the fire engine we had a lift on, as well as the present members.

The other visits were to the de Vries family, where I met Bob and Nancy, the son and daughter; I also met the Christen family, the father and mother, and two of the children, Pim and Niki.

These visits were a real pleasure, very nostalgic and emotional, but it was also nice to realise how much the R.A.F. is appreciated in Holland. At least they were and still are grateful for our efforts. I was delighted to hear that every year on the anniversary of the National Liberation Day (5th May), the Dutch children of all the towns, large and small, visit the graves of all the airmen and place flowers as a token of thanks.

I am glad to end my experiences in a note of pleasure. I myself have now retired after many years in accountancy and enjoy life to the full with my family.

I still feel very, very thankful for the help and unselfish sacrifices given to me by so many good people over those seven years. I only wish the same attitude and state of mind could exist today, and not the constant antagonism; but never mind, such is life and as the old saying goes: *"Your life is your own to make or mar"*.

FOOTNOTE

Since compiling these memoirs I have regretfully received the sad news that three of my helpers have passed away. Mr and Mrs Piet Christen and Bob de Vries, who were typical examples of the Dutch people who faced adversity with great courage and did all in their power to help the war effort in what ever way possible.

EJB

APPENDIX ONE

RECOMMENDATIONS FOR HONOURS AND AWARDS.

Christian Names ......ERIC JAMES............Surname....BLAKEMORE.....
Rank...........SERGEANT.............Official No..914262........
Command or Group ....NO. 3 GROUP........Unit...NO. 9 SQUADRON........

	Since outbreak of War.	Since last Award.
Total Hours flown on Operations	172.55.	N/A.
Number of sorties carried out	30	"

Recognition for which recommended ....Distinguished Flying Medal....
Appointment held ....Wireless Operator/Air Gunner........

Particulars of meritorious service for which the recommendation is made. Including date and place.

On the night of 29th August, 1941, Sgt. BLAKEMORE was the front gunner in Wellington R.1279 which was detailed to attack a target in MANNHEIM. The bombs were dropped in the target area at 0015 hours, after which the aircraft entered cloud at 12,000 ft. In taking evasive action from flak the pilot lost control of the aircraft, which turned over onto its back. The Captain of the aircraft told the crew to prepare to abandon aircraft. Unfortunately, through some misunderstanding, the Navigator and first Wireless Operator actually did abandon the aircraft before the pilot regained control at a height of 2,000 ft. By this time, Sgt. BLAKEMORE, realizing that the safe return of the aircraft would be largely dependent on wireless aid, had already taken the first operator's place and was endeavouring to establish W/T. communication. All the M/F. coils had fallen out of the aircraft while it was out of control. After some time, Sgt. BLAKEMORE managed to get into communication with HONINGTON H/F M/F Station and successfully obtained homing bearings which brought the aircraft safely to its base.

Though Sgt BLAKEMORE knew that all the navigation instruments except one map had been lost and also all the W/T.M/F coils had been lost, these major difficulties in making a safe return only incited him to great efforts and with estimable coolness and patience he was eventually successful. His work gave confidence to the remaining members of the crew, and was material in bringing the aircraft safely to base.

Sgt. BLAKEMORE has completed successfully thirty major operational flights against the enemy, including one to BERLIN. His cheerful disposition and determination in flying against the enemy has been an example of the highest order to the other members of the Squadron, and he is strongly recommended for the award of the Distinguished Flying Medal.

17th October, 1941.

WING COMMANDER, COMMANDING
NO. 9 SQUADRON, HONINGTON.

Covering remarks of Station Commander.

The Award of the D.F.M. to the above mentioned airman is strongly recommended.

Date. 19. 10. 41

GROUP CAPTAIN, COMMANDING
R.A.F. STATION, HONINGTON.

Covering remarks of Air Officer Commanding.

I concur in the above recommendation and consider that this Wireless Operator/Air Gunner has shown initiative and coolness in an emergency which fully justifies his being considered for special recognition.

28/10/41.

Air Vice-Marshal,

DAILY EXPRESS
Tuesday, December 23rd, 1941

The man who did not bale out

TOLD by the Air Ministry last night was the story of the Man Who Did Not Bale Out. It was told in an account of how he won the Distinguished Flying Medal.

He is Sergeant Eric James Blakemore, of No. 9 Squadron, a 22-year-old Bournemouth man, an accountant before he enlisted in February last year as a radio operator-air gunner.

One night last August he was front gunner of an aircraft detailed to attack Mannheim. After the target area had been bombed Blakemore's pilot, while avoiding flak, lost control and the aircraft turned on its back when 12,000 feet up.

INSTRUMENTS LOST

The pilot regained control at 2,000 feet, but, because of a misunderstanding, the navigator and first radio operator had baled out.

Blakemore realised that the safe return of the aircraft would be largely dependent on radio help, especially as many navigating instruments had been lost.

So he took the first operator's place. With great skill, coolness, and perseverance he got in radio touch with his base and obtained bearings which enabled the pilot to fly home safely.

"His work," the Air Ministry said, "installed confidence in his comrades, and most certainly greatly assisted in their ultimate safety."

Blakemore has been in 31 bombing attacks.

NEWS CHRONICLE
Tuesday, December 23rd, 1941

Sergeant Eric James Blakemore, who receives the D.F.M., was front gunner in a plane attacking Mannheim. The machine turned over at 12,000ft. Control was regained at 2,000ft., but the navigator and first radio operator had baled out.

Blakemore took the operator's place, and his work brought the plane home.

BOURNEMOUTH DAILY ECHO
Tuesday, December 23rd, 1941

HOW HE WON D.F.M.

Bournemouth Man's Great Daring

IN one account of how a Bournemouth man won the Distinguished Flying Medal, the Air Ministry have just published a stirring story.

The man is Sergeant Eric James Blakemore, of No. 9 Squadron, a 22 years old local man, an accountant before he enlisted in February last year as a radio operator-air gunner.

One night last August he was front gunner of an aircraft detailed to attack Mannheim. After the target area had been bombed, Blakemore's pilot, while avoiding flak, lost control, and the aircraft turned on its back when 12,000 feet up.

COOLNESS AND SKILL

The pilot regained control at 2,000 feet, but, because of a misunderstanding, the navigator and first radio operator had baled out.

Blakemore realised that the safe return of the aircraft would be largely dependent on radio help, especially as many navigating instruments had been lost.

So he took the first operator's place. With great skill, coolness and perseverance he got in radio touch with his base and obtained bearings which enabled the pilot to fly home safely.

"His work," the Air Ministry said, "installed confidence in his comrades, and most certainly greatly assisted in their ultimate safety."

Blakemore has been in 31 bombing attacks.

APPENDIX TWO

THE BOURNEMOUTH DAILY ECHO
Monday, May 11th, 1942

"D.F.M. FOR GREAT SKILL"

Sergt. Eric James Blakemore, R.A.F., aged 22, of 30, Saxonhurst-road, Bournemouth, and of No. 9 Squadron, who won the D.F.M. "for great skill, coolness and perseverance following an attack on Mannheim." While avoiding flak the sergeants' pilot lost control and the aircraft turned on its back and dropped 10,000 feet.

King Decorates War Heroes

AIRMAN'S PARENTS' DESCRIPTION

Former residents of Wood Green and Southgate, Mr. and Mrs. F. W. Blakemore describe their experiences of an investiture recently held by the King at Buckingham Palace at which their only son, Sergeant Eric Blakemore, R.A.F., aged 22, was presented with the Distinguished Flying Medal.

Relatives and friends of the many war heroes were directed to their seats by members of the Home Guard. There were a good number of children present.

The King, dressed in naval uniform, decorated the recipients from a small platform erected at the side of a gallery. An army officer, standing at the King's right hand, called out the individual names of those entitled to an award. Those named immediately approached the King, turned to face the King, bowed, and took two steps forward. After clipping the decoration on to the uniform or dress, His Majesty shook hands with the recipient and spoke a few words of congratulation and good wishes. In some cases he had a short chat and asked questions. The recipient then stepped backwards two paces, bowed again and, turning, left by the opposite gangway.

An orchestra played the National Anthem at the beginning and end of the ceremony, and also throughout the presentation played light incidental music.

The investiture took about one hour and over a hundred men and women were decorated.

APPENDIX THREE

<u>NIGHT RAID REPORT NO. 639</u>
<u>COPY NO. 22</u>

<u>BOMBER COMMAND REPORT ON NIGHT OPERATIONS.
21/22nd JUNE 1944.
WESSELING ; SCHOLVEN-BUER ; BERLIN ; Minelaying.</u>

<u>SUMMARY</u>
1. 265 Lancasters and Mosquitos were despatched against the synthetic oil plants at Wesseling and Scholven-Buer; but both were covered with thick low cloud, and neither was seriously damaged. Fighters found our aircraft easy targets against the bright midsummer sky, and 45 bombers were lost. Fighters and minelayers operated without loss, and Mosquitos attacked Berlin.

<u>WEATHER FORECAST</u>
2. Bases: Low stratus will become widespread after dusk, S. of the Humber. Good diversions in S.W. and N.W.
   Continent: Ruhr will remain clear all night. Paris will have little cloud until after midnight. Pase de Calais will have 10/10ths low stratus after 0200.

WESSELING : SCHOLVEN-BUER.

<u>PLANS OF ATTACK</u>
3. <u>Wesseling</u>. 5 Group visual marking. The target was to be illuminated with flares, in the light of which Mosquitos were to drop red spot fires on the A/P. If accurate, these were to be backed up with more red spot fires, and green and red T.I. Yellows were to be used to cancel wide markers. Main force crews were to aim the

centre bomb of each stick at the centre of all visible markers, unless otherwise ordered by the Controller. If no markers were visible, crews were not to wait, but were to bomb on H2S. H = 0132. Main force: H + 8 to H + 17. Bombing height: 17 -22.000'.

4. Scholven-Buer. OBOE groundmarking, assisted by 5 Group visual marking. The same method as for Wesseling, except that 5 OBOE Mosquitos were to open the attack by dropping yellow T.I. The visual Mosquitos were then to mark the A/P with red spot fires by flarelight. H = 0132. Bombing height: 17 - 20.000'.

	WESS.	SCH. -BUER
SORTIES		
5. No. of aircraft despatched	133	132
" " " reporting attack on primary area	124	125
" " " reporting attack on alternative area	1	-
" " " abortive sorties	8	7
" " " missing	37 (27.8%)	8 (6.1%)

WEATHER EXPERIENCED

6. Bases: Low stratus became widespread after dusk.
   Wesseling and Scholven-Buer: 10/10ths cloud, tops 3.000'; no moon. 10/10ths over whole route.

NARRATIVE OF ATTACKS

7. Neither attack can be described in detail,

since the thick cloud prevented all but a very few aircraft from photographing ground detail. At both targets crews attacked on the glow of markers.

DAY RECONNAISSANCE
8. The only apparent damage caused to either target affected an oil storage tank in the N.W. corner of the Wesseling plant, which suffered from blast.

ENEMY DEFENCES
9. These operations were carried out without the assistance of supporting diversions or the MANDREL SCREEN. Our aircraft all took the same route as far as a point N. of Gilze Rijen, and then diverged to their respective targets. The enemy controllers plotted our bombers from the Hague, and concentrated almost all their fighters on the southerly (Wesseling) force. The brightness of the moonless sky - it was midsummer night - was undoubtedly the chief cause of the unusual measure of success obtained by the fighters. Intense flak was met at both targets, accurately predicted up to 18 - 20.000'. There is no evidence that our bombers destroyed any fighters.

CASUALTIES
10.   7 of the 37 losses incurred on Wesseling were attributed to heavy flak, 2 bombers falling at the target and the others to defences on track, mostly located at airfields. The remaining 30 missing aircraft cannot be fully accounted for, and, while it is presumed that fighters were responsible for nearly all, only 18 can confidently be traced to this cause. Of the 8 aircraft lost on Scholven, 5 were destroyed in combat and 3 by flak. One aircraft

of each force sustained irreparable damage from fighters. No landing or taxying accidents occurred.

BERLIN

11. 32 Mosquitos were despatched against Berlin. Some markers were accurate but others were scattered. 30 Mosquitos attacked. Many fires were seen burning from the daylight raid of VIII-U.S.B.C. The remaining 2 aircraft bombed Kiel. No aircraft was lost; but 3 were hit by flak, 1 seriously.

MINELAYING

12. 13 Stirlings laid 65 mines off N.W. France without incident.

FIGHTERS AND SPECIAL OPERATIONS.

13. 58 Mosquitos from 100 Group and A.D.G.B. were active on SERRATE and intruder patrols. They destroyed 1 Do.-217 and damaged a He.-177 and an U/I aircraft.
10 Halifaxes made special sorties. All returned safely.

MLM/JT.
MC/S.26342/2/ORS4,
18th. October 1944.

APPENDIX FOUR

No.50 Squadron,
Royal Air Force,
Skellingthorpe,
Lincoln.

Reference:-
50S/643/351/P.1.

22nd June, 1944.

Dear Mr Blakemore,

  It is with deep regret that I have to confirm that your son, Pilot Officer E.J. Blakemore, has been reported missing from operations carried out on the night of 21/22nd June, 1944.

  He was the Wireless Operator of a Lancaster aircraft, captained by Squadron Leader T.B.Cole, which was detailed to attack targets at BUER, and, unfortunately, nothing further has been heard of the aircraft since take-off.

  There is always the possibility that he made a safe parachute landing and may be a prisoner of war, in which case you will either hear from him direct or from the Air Ministry, who will receive advice from the International Red Cross Committee. In either case, it will be some considerable time before any news is received; i.e. from two to three months.

  It is desired to explain that the request in the telegram notifying you of the casualty to your son, was included with the object of avoiding his chance of escape being prejudiced by undue publicity in case he was still at large. This is not to say that any information about him is available, but is a precaution adopted in the case of all personnel reported missing.

  This was your son's eighth sortie on his second tour of operations and he was a most experienced and competent Wireless Operator. He was popular with the crew and will be greatly missed by his comrades on the Squadron.

  With/...

TELEPHONE: GERRARD 9234
Extn...............
Any communications on the
subject of this letter should
be addressed to :—
THE
UNDER SECRETARY
OF STATE,
and the following number
quoted :— P.419075/5/P.4.(B4)
Your Ref ....

AIR MINISTRY
(Casualty Branch),
73-77, OXFORD STREET,
W.1.

23 November, 1944

Sir,

    I am directed to refer to a letter from this Department dated 31st August, 1944, concerning your son, Flying Officer Eric James Blakemore, Royal Air Force, and to inform you that a further report has now been received from the International Red Cross Committee, Geneva, which states that Sergeant Shorter and the one unknown member of the crew were buried on 23rd June, 1944, in Graves numbered 704 and 705 respectively in the Parish Cemetery at Epe.

    As there are two places of this name, one in Holland and one in Germany, a special enquiry as to its precise location has been made to the International Red Cross Committee, Geneva, and you will be notified when this information comes to hand.

    It is regretted that it is still not possible to state precisely who is the one that is unidentified, but the report is forwarded for your information.

    I am again to express the sincere sympathy of the Department with you in your prolonged anxiety and to assure you that any further news received will be immediately forwarded to you.

I am, Sir,
Your obedient Servant,

[signature]

for Director of Personal Services.

F.W. Blakemore, Esq.,
30, Saxonhurst Road,
Ensbury Park,
Bournemouth,
Hampshire.

APPENDIX FIVE

Letter received from Mrs. Segar containing information confirming the author was still alive

"Whitwell"
6 Manor Rd.
Itchen
Southampton.

27-11-44.

Dear Friend,

Firstly I must explain to you that I was an English resident in Holland up to July of this year, since when I have been repatriated to England from an internment camp in France. On my departure from German occupied Holland which part unfortunately is still under German rule. I was asked to convey to you by a very good Dutch friend of mine that, date not fallen into enemy hands. In all probability you have had confirmation of this good news from another source or perhaps he has since managed to contact with our own forces operating in the neighbourhood.

I conclude with my best wishes for his wellbeing and a speedy reunion.

With Kind Regards
Yours Sincerely
(Mrs) F. E. A. Segar.

Telephone No.: GERRARD 9234
Trunk Calls and Telegraphic Address:
"AIR MINISTRY," LONDON

AIR MINISTRY,
(Casualty Branch),
73-77 OXFORD STREET,
LONDON, W.1

P.419075/5/P.4.B.3.

7th December, 1944.

Sir,

    I am directed to refer to your letter dated the 29th November, 1944, and to thank you for forwarding a copy of the letter received from Mrs. Segar.

    I am to advise you that confirmation has been received that your son, Flying Officer Eric James Blakemore, Royal Air Force, was in enemy occupied territory but not in enemy hands, during November.

    You are advised to continue to treat this news as confidential pending further information or of your son's arrival in Allied hands.

    You are assured that any further news received will be immediately passed to you.

    I am, Sir,
        Your obedient Servant,

        S. L. Baker.

    for Director of Personal Services.

F.W. Blakemore, Esq.,
  30, Saxonhurst Road,
    Ensbury Park,
      Bournemouth,
        Hants.

APPENDIX SIX

Extract from Epe Fire Brigade Records
re. escape from Apeldoorn

Sunday, october 1, 1944.

14.30 a.m. False fire-alarm in the neighbourhood of Vossenbroek.

Publication in a newspaper, february 1946.

EPE
Assistance to allied aviators.

Some of our fellow-citizens already received expressions of gratitude for assisting allied fliers who crashed or had to make a forced landing..
One of these days this also happened to 3 members of the fire-brigade of Epe who - conducted by commander G. Kwakkel - picked up 3 British fliers somewhere near Vaassen and delivered them, camouflaged as firemen, safely at the meeting-place in Nunspeet.
A heroic stunt that is worth telling. It is a pity that only e few times the local circumstances allowed the fire-brigade to exploit this great possibility.

Part of the minutes of the fire-brigade meeting of june 1945.
Report of what really happened on october 1, 1944.

On sunday our co-operation was requested in connection with the transportation of 3 British aviators who were coming from Apeldoorn along the canal-dike and had to be accompanied to Nunspeet.
Three members of the fire-brigade - with the necessary clothing, like coats and helmets - left for the canal near Zuuk at break-neck speed, then on along the canal heading for Apeldoorn where the fliers were picked up. At even higher speed they returned to Epe via Emst. It all worked out nicely, excellent work !, but very dangerous indeed in view of the occupation by the SD and more of that scum.
Anyway, the 3 British fliers were saved and stayed free from imprisonment.

APPENDIX SEVEN

I.S.9.(W.E.A.)

WARNING AGAINST GIVING INFORMATION ABOUT YOUR ESCAPE OR HOW YOU EVADED CAPTURE

This applies to Members of all Services and continues even after discharge therefrom.

1. It is the duty of all persons to safeguard information which might either directly or indirectly, be useful to the enemy.

2. The Defence Regulations make it an offence, punishable with imprisonment, to publish or to communicate to any unauthorised person any information or anything which purports to be information on any matter which would or might be directly or indirectly useful to the enemy.

3. This document is brought to your personal notice so that you may clearly understand information about your escape or how you evaded capture is information which would be useful to the enemy, and that therefore to communicate any information about your escape or how you evaded capture is an offence under the Defence Regulations.

4. You must not disclose the names of those who helped you, the method or methods by which you escaped, the route you followed or how you reached this country, nor must you even give information of such a general nature as the names of the countries through which you travelled. All such information may be of assistance to the enemy and a danger to your friends. **Be specially on your guard with persons who may be newspaper representatives.**

5. **Publishing or communicating information includes**:—

    (a) publication of accounts of your experiences in books, newspapers or periodicals (including Regimental Journals), wireless broadcasts or lectures ;

and   (b) giving information to friends and acquaintances either male or female, in private letters, in casual conversations or discussions, even if these friends or acquaintances are in H.M.'s or Allied Forces and however " safe " you may consider them to be.

6. F.O. (S57-44)
   A.C.I. (1896-43) } prohibit lecturing by escapers or evaders to any unit without
   A.M.C.O. A89-44   prior permission of the Admiralty, War Office, Air Ministry.

TO BE COMPLETED IN THE PERSON'S OWN HANDWRITING.

I have read this document and understand that if I disclose information about my escape, evasion of capture I am liable to disciplinary action.

Signed _Eric J. Blakemore_   Date _11/3/45_

Full Name (Block letters) _ERIC JAMES BLAKEMORE_

Rank and Number _F/O 169156_

Unit _50 SQDN 5 GROUP_

Witnessed by _____

APPENDIX EIGHT

BOURNEMOUTH DAILY ECHO
Friday, March 16th, 1945

ON HIS WAY HOME
After Hiding in Enemy Territory

"HOME safe. See you soon," was the wording of a telegram received on Tuesday by Mr. and Mrs. F. W. Blakemore Saxonhurst-road, Bournemouth, from their only son, Flying Officer Eric Blakemore, D.F.M.

It was the first time they had heard from him for nine months. For long he was hiding in enemy territory.

"We always felt that he was still alive ", Mr. Blakemore told the "Daily Echo".

In June 1944 Mr. and Mrs. Blakemore received word from the Air Ministry that their son was missing following operations over Germany.

Later the Air Ministry confirmed the news, and stated that two members of the crew one of whom was unidentified had been killed and that three members had been made prisoners of war.

FORTY MISSIONS

Blakemore had then completed over forty flights over enemy country.

In November, 1944, Mr. and Mrs. Blakemore received a letter from a person who had escaped from German territory in the previous July and who only a week previous to writing arrived in England. The letter stated that a Mr. Eric Blakemore, of Saxonhurst-road, Bournemouth, was safe and well. This information was confirmed when the person called to see Mr. and Mrs. Blakemore at their home. Although the person had not seen Flying Officer Blakemore there was doubt that he was alive and well—hiding in enemy territory.

F.O. Blakemore won the D.F.M. while serving under the late Group Captain Pickard.

LONDON EVENING STANDARD
Wednesday, March 14th, 1945

Master Bomber Hid In Germany For Months

After hiding in enemy territory for a long time after his Lancaster master-bomber was brought down over Germany, Flying Officer Eric Blakemore, D.F.M., of Wood Green, Middlesex, has arrived safely in England.

He was reported missing ten minths ago, and the first his parents had heard from him in that time was a telegram yesterday.

Last November a mysterious person who had escaped from Germany called at his parents' Bournemouth home and said he was safe, and in hiding. Two members of the crew of the Lancaster were killed, and three were captured.

THE GUARDIAN
Friday, April 20th, 1945

In Germany, but Never a P.O.W.

The adventures of 26-years-old Flying Officer E. J. Blakemore, D.F.M.—a well-known Timperley boy—will have to remain unwritten until the "cease fire" with Germany is given. Eric recently arrived home from Germany, whence he made good his escape and, apparently, according to all reports, has never been a prisoner of war.

In June, 1944, Eric's machine (a Lancaster bomber) was brought down over Germany. All the crew baled out, but three were killed and three taken prisoners. Although Eric landed within a short distance of his plane and, with his own eyes, saw it go up in flames, he was able to contact only one other member of his crew.

He was officially posted as missing, and his parents heard nothing of him until they received a letter in November, 1944, from a complete stranger who wrote: "I have managed to escape from Germany, and have news of a Mr. Eric Blakemore who is safe and well."

"This astounding communication was closely followed by a visit from a foreigner who told them that, although he had not met their son he was, at the time of his leaving Germany, safe and well and had managed to evade falling into the hands of the Germans.

Again there was silence, and the suspense was broken by a telegram from Eric early last month which read: "Home safe. See you soon." The "Guardian" is informed by his parents that Eric made many attempts to cross the Rhine, and finally succeeded in reaching the Allied lines safely. What he did and how he did it is a story that will have to be narrated at some future date.

WITH "F. FOR FREDDIE"
Flying-Officer Blakemore was awarded the D.F.M. (earlier reported in the "Guardian") in 1942, while serving under the late Group Captain Percy Pickard, of "F. for Freddie—Target for to-night" fame, and, along with Group Captain Pickard and others, was included in a painting for the War Office by Mr. T. C. Dugdale, R.A.

Before joining the R.A.F., in February, 1940, Eric lived in Stockport Road, Timperley, but his parents have now made their home in the South of England, and it is their intention to again visit the Altrincham district shortly.

APPENDIX NINE

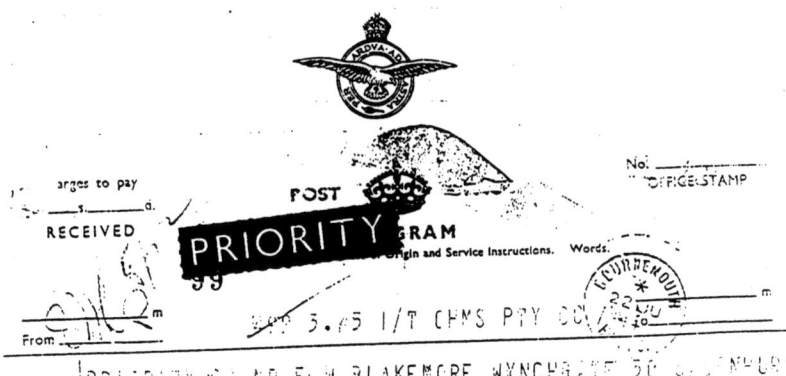

POST OFFICE PRIORITY TELEGRAM

Charges to pay
RECEIVED
From

PRIORITY-CC MR F W BLAKEMORE WYNCHGATE 30 SACONHURST
RD ENSBURY PARK BOURNEMOUTH =
22ND JUNE REGRET TO INFORM YOU THAT YOUR SON
PILOTOFFICER ERIC JAMES BLAKEMORE IS MISSING AS THE
RESULT OF AIR OPERATIONS ON THE NIGHT OF 21/22 JUNE
1942 STOP LETTER FOLLOWS STOP ANY FURTHER INFORMATION
RECEIVED WILL BE IMMEDIATELY COMMUNICATED TO YOU STOP ms
PENDING RECEIPT OF WRITTEN NOTIFICATION FROM THE AIRMINISTRY

POST OFFICE TELEGRAM

Charges to pay
RECEIVED
No. 888 OFFICE STAMP
Prefix. Time handed in. Office of Origin and Service Instructions. Words.
52
352 8.11 LONDON C.O CHMS 22
From
To

MR AND MRS F W BLAKEMORE WYNCHGATE 30 SACONHURST,
RD ENSBURY PARK BOURNEMOUTH HANTS
= HOME SAFE HOPE TO SEE YOU SOON = ERIC + +

+ 30 +

For free repetition of doubtful words telephone "TELEGRAMS ENQUIRY" or call, with this form at office of delivery. Other enquiries should be accompanied by this form and, if possible, the envelope